D E S E R T
DESIGNS

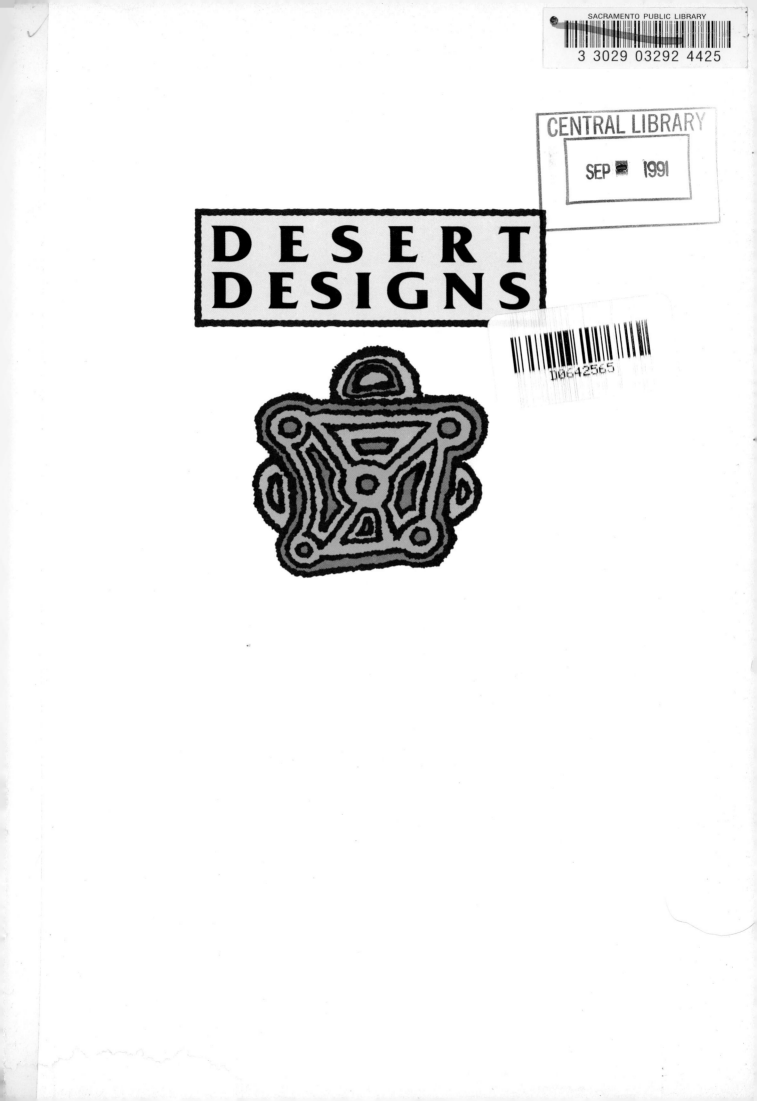

DESERT DESIGNS

26 Knits by Aboriginal Artists

Text by Stephen Muecke

Photography by Grant Matthews

Prentice Hall Press

Prentice Hall Press
15 Columbus Circle
New York, New York 10023

First published in Australasia in 1990 by
Simon & Schuster Australia
7 Grosvenor Place, Brookvale NSW 2100

PRENTICE HALL PRESS and colophons are trademarks of
Simon & Schuster, Inc.

ISBN: 0-13-200734-7

Designed by Deborah Brash / Brash Design
Sketches for patterns by Robyn Malcolm
Patterns and graphs by Katherine Jarvis and Sue Morton
Typeset in Australia by Savage Type Pty Ltd
Produced by Mandarin Offset in Hong Kong

The background design on the cover and throughout
the book is by Deborah Brash and based on the Jimmy
Pike design *Larripuka*.

Note: The views expressed in the foreword do not necessarily
reflect those of the Australia Council.

CONTENTS

FOREWORD 6 ▪ INTRODUCTION 7
THE DESERT DESIGNS COMPANY 8
GENERAL INSTRUCTIONS 9

JIMMY PIKE

Larripuka 12
Country 16
Mangkaja — White Bird 19
Partiri — Desert Flowers 22
Two Little Girls 26
Flowers After the Rain 30
Kartiya Boat 33
Kurntumaru and Parnaparnti 36

DEAGGIDDITT

Emu — Bush Food 42
Papatjara — Dingoes 46
Mamu — Spirit 49
Kukaku — Hunting Time 52
Mother and Baby 56
Kalya — Emu Chicks 59
Seven Emu Sisters 62
Maratjara — Many Hands 65
Didjeridoo Player 69
Marlu — Kangaroo 72
Mara — Hand 76

DORIS GINGINGARA

Leaves and Tracks 82
Batjikala — Long Pipe 85
Barramundi 88
Djarram — Tree Bark Nets 92
Rainstorm Magic 95
Kingirama — Grinding Stones 98
Batjikala — The Totems 101

FOREWORD

As an admirer of Jimmy Pike and the unique role he plays in Australian cultural life, it is a pleasure to write a foreword for a book featuring Jimmy Pike and his fellow artists Deaggidditt and Doris Gingingara.

The artists featured in **Desert Designs** are in a sense pioneers. Each has chosen to forego the world of official Aboriginal affairs patronage and government funding in favour of dealing directly with the world of commerce.

Any improvement in the living conditions of Aborigines, and their acceptance as the first Australians, will only occur when all Australians make Aboriginal rights a concern in the same way that an increasing number have taken the environmental cause to heart. Books such as **Desert Designs** will play an important role in doing this by alerting and sensitising Australians to the living culture of Aboriginal Australia.

One of the reasons for the book's excellence is, I believe, the creative tension that results when an accommodation is sought between the demands of the market place and the Aboriginality of the artists. The motifs and symbols featured in **Desert Designs** are uniformly strong. In association with the knit patterns, they translate into an authentic Australian fashion which combines contemporary urban aesthetics with the roots of Aboriginal culture. The concerns of the artists range from the metaphysical to the domestic and bring meaning once more into modern design. More importantly, they allow the wearers of these knits access to the world of traditional Aboriginal Australia where art and life, man and nature, are one.

Philip Morrissey O.A.M.
Programme Manager
Aboriginal Arts Unit
Australia Council

INTRODUCTION

DESERT DESIGNS is a book of authentically Australian knits designed by Aboriginal artists. It includes patterns for sweaters, cardigans and vests for both men and women, that are ideal for knitters of all standards. Not only does **Desert Designs** give you the opportunity to create your own Aboriginal knits, but also to learn something about the culture that has inspired them.

The designs in this book are the work of three artists: Jimmy Pike, Doris Gingingara and Deaggidditt. Drawing on the traditions of their ancient cultures, the artists have created designs which reflect their relationship with the land, their nomadic lifestyle and the whole spiritual realm known as 'the Dreaming'. Jimmy Pike lives in the Great Sandy Desert in Australia's far north-west. He is an accomplished painter whose inspiration comes from the land around him. Doris Gingingara and Deaggidditt come from very different parts of the country and this is reflected in their art. Doris was brought up in Arnhem Land in the same region as the tropical Kakadu National Park, while Deaggidditt is from the Western Desert, a much drier region.

With every pattern there is a photograph of the original artwork from which the designs have been developed. The artist talks about each of the designs and there is an accompanying explanation to give you more information about Aboriginal culture. Sometimes the artists have drawn on scenes from everyday life and their designs show people hunting and playing the didjeridoo. Other designs draw upon ancient and traditional forms of art — rock paintings and wood carvings — while still others translate the artists' personal experiences with the mythology so vital to Aboriginal culture. Their art also represents their perceptions of the land around them, from the dry desert to the abundance of life after the seasonal rains.

Art in Aboriginal society is art for everyone, an essential part of everyday life. Jimmy Pike, Doris Gingingara and Deaggidditt have done more than just repeat the styles of their cultural tradition. They have made Aboriginal art accessible to everyone. The knits in this book give you the opportunity to make art a part of your everyday life, whether you are interested in the Australian landscape, Aboriginal society or authentically Australian design.

Photograph courtesy of Sheridan

THE DESERT DESIGNS COMPANY

THE DESERT DESIGNS company began in the early 1980s, the inspiration of two young art teachers, Stephen Culley and David Wroth. Contact with Western Australian Aboriginal culture in the Kimberleys had left an impression on them both that there was a rich heritage of art largely unknown to the wider community. After leaving the bush, they returned to the city and this impression was reinforced in art classes held for Aboriginal prisoners at Fremantle.

Stephen Culley and David Wroth formed the Desert Designs company to open a commercial avenue for some of the exciting art they had encountered. They were also keen to challenge the accepted understanding of the place of Aboriginal art in Australian society. For Aboriginal artists working in innovative areas there had been little scope in the established art market. The Desert Designs company aimed to provide an example of how Aboriginal artists could earn a living from their art and change the directions of their lives.

Jimmy Pike was the first artist to join the Desert Designs company. His creative strength and natural artistic ability were immediately obvious to Culley and Wroth. Pike was working with texta-pens — an impermanent medium. Culley and Wroth were determined to save his art from disappearing. Another of Pike's strengths was his ability to communicate the stories of his people. So, in 1985, the Desert Designs company began translating the work of Jimmy Pike on to fabric — a natural progression from his silk-screen and lino-cut prints. Not only was it important that the designs be reproduced but also that people understood them. From the beginning, the stories were an integral part of the designs.

As more artists have joined the company, the Desert Designs products have come to reflect a wider view of Australia from the perspective of different Aboriginal cultures. There are the differing responses to Western society and varying interpretations of the extremes of the Australian landscape.

Based in Perth, Western Australia, the Desert Designs company was isolated from the fashion centres of Sydney and Melbourne, and needed to find an Australian manufacturer who could also distribute the garments. In 1986, the Byers Company in Sydney began producing the first national range of Desert Designs garments. It was an immediate success and it was not long before the designs had been taken up by other manufacturers and a full range of products were on the market. After success in Australia, the marketing was extended to Japan, Europe and the United States. The Desert Designs company has established itself as a leading design house and is contributing to the continuing growth and success of Aboriginal art.

GENERAL INSTRUCTIONS

Tension or Gauge

The **tension** or **gauge** of a knitted garment refers to the number of stitches measured horizontally and the number of rows measured vertically over a specific area of knitting — most often 10 cm by 10 cm (4 ins by 4 ins).

Sometimes only the number of stitches is referred to, as in this book. **It is very important that you achieve the tension given for each pattern**, otherwise the size and shape of the garment may differ dramatically from the pattern.

Before starting any garment, knit a sample square slightly larger than the area stated in the pattern, using the needles, yarn and stitch required. Lay the finished square flat, without stretching. Measure 10 cm by 10 cm (4 ins by 4 ins) and mark out with pins. Count the number of stitches between the pins. If the number is larger than that stated in the pattern, your tension is too loose; you will need to use smaller needles to achieve the correct tension. If the number of stitches is fewer, your tension is too tight; you will need to use larger needles to achieve the correct tension.

Reading the Graphs

Except where otherwise indicated, when working from graphs, read odd numbered rows (knit rows) from right to left and even numbered rows (purl rows) from left to right. One square represents one stitch.

Changing Colours

When changing colours in the centre of a row, twist the colour to be used underneath and to the right of the colour just used, making sure that both yarns are worked firmly at joins. Always change colours on the wrong side of the work so that the change does not show. Use a separate ball of yarn for each section of colour. Wind a quantity of yarn around a bobbin and place the end through the slot to hold. Unwind only enough yarn to knit the required stitches, then place yarn in the slot, keeping the bobbin close to the work.

Making Up

Care taken in putting together the knitted pieces will result in a better looking garment.

If you wish to press them into shape, you should first check whether there is specific ironing information on the yarn ball band. Most woollen yarns can be safely pressed **lightly** on the **wrong** side, using 'wool' setting. If in doubt, cover the pieces with a damp cloth before pressing. Do **not** stretch.

An alternative is to lightly dampen the pieces, gently pull them into shape, and lay them flat to dry.

The pieces should be laid flat when matching up seams.

If pinning seams before sewing up, start by pinning each end, and work towards the middle. Use the yarn knitted with to sew up the garment. Sew seams in the order indicated in the pattern. Yarn ends should be 'woven' into the back of the work using a wool needle, before being trimmed. Where more than one colour has been used, weave the ends of each into its own colour area.

Garment Care

A hand-knitted garment needs special but simple care. It is best to follow cleaning instructions on the yarn ball band, though the following instructions are suitable for most woollen yarns.

There are a number of washing liquids and powders specially developed for washing wool and which are widely available. Always use one of these for washing your garment. Do not wash woollens in hot water, use only cold or warm water. Check that the powder or liquid is completely dissolved before putting the garment in the water. Do not run the tap directly onto the garment.

Rinse the garment thoroughly but carefully. Do not wring — to remove excess water place the garment in a pillowslip and spin in a washing machine for no more than a few minutes.

To dry, lay the garment flat on a towel, away from direct sunlight. Do not dry in front of any kind of direct heat — such as a fire or heater — this can damage the fibres.

Abbreviations

K	knit
P	purl
MC	main colour
C1, C2 etc.	first colour, second colour etc.
st st	stocking stitch
sts	stitches
patt	pattern
beg	beginning
foll	following
rep	repeat
cont	continue
rem	remaining
alt	alternate
inc	increase
dec	decrease
yfwd	yarn forward, bring yarn to front of work before knitting next stitch
ybk	yarn back; take yarn to back of work
K2tog	knit two stitches together

Knitting Needle Sizes

English	000	00	0	1	2	3	4	5	6	7	8	9	10	11	12	13	14
Metric	10	9	8	7.5	7	6.5	6	5.5	5	4.5	4	3.75	3.25	3	2.75	2.25	2
American	15	13	12	11	10½	10	9	8	7	6	5	4	3	2	1	1	00

Note: All needle sizes are given in metric and then in English sizes.

COUNTRY

JIMMY PIKE

JIMMY PIKE lives in a bush camp on the edge of the Great Sandy Desert. There he paints and produces the designs for which he has become so well known. He spends much of his time hunting and exploring the desert he knew as a child.

Born in remote sandhill country a long way south of his present camp, Jimmy was a member of one of the last groups of people to leave the desert and settle on cattle stations in the Kimberleys during the 1950s. He spent his childhood as a nomad, moving with his family around the various waterholes that were the focal points of their arid country, occasionally visiting related groups of people in adjacent territory. His language is *Walmatjarri*. He learnt the arts of tracking and hunting, and can find his way unerringly around the vast and — to European eyes — featureless country to which he belongs. He knows not only the physical characteristics of the natural world about him, but also their spiritual significance and the age-old *Walmatjarri* ceremonies which celebrated them. The *Walmatjarri* people expressed themselves artistically through ceremonial bodypainting and decorative carving.

After leaving the desert as a youth,

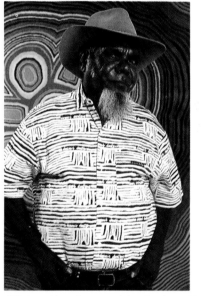

Jimmy Pike soon started work as a stockman, learning to ride horses and manage cattle. He mastered many new skills, and worked for a number of years on cattle stations, and later in towns, in the Kimberleys. For many years Jimmy Pike supplemented his earnings by carving and selling artifacts. It wasn't until 1981 that he was first introduced to Western-style painting and discovered his talent for art and design. A few years later he set up his isolated camp in the desert, not far from the route he and his relatives travelled on their first journey north. He works in the open, resting his paintings on a rough work table he made for himself from old planks. He stores his art and other materials under a heavy canvas fly, where he also takes refuge from the rare but heavy seasonal falls of rain. On journeys south from his camp, following mining tracks, he has rediscovered and dug out many of the waterholes he knew in his youth. With other members of his family he hopes eventually to visit all the principal waterholes of the country in which he grew up, the country from whose ancient culture come the stories and symbols that inspire Jimmy Pike's art.   P. A. LOWE

JIMMY PIKE

Larripuka

Larripuka

'In the Dreamtime a big mob of people been travelling east through Larripuka country, right through to Japingka. That's the story of old people. Law country and Dreamtime country. The Law is passed from grandfather to father to son. When all the people finished travelling east, they leave Jila [*waterhole*], Jilji [*sandhill*] *and* Ngapa [*water*].

'Before, people been live in the country and people been die in the country, long time ago. People move around, rainy time, and when it come winter time, they move back again.'

Jimmy Pike's story summarises two aspects of Aboriginal nomadism. First there were the ancestral heroes, in the Dreamtime, who travelled on particular tracks, creating landforms and giving man laws, language and ceremony. Today the holders of these traditions follow the same tracks seasonally, arriving in places at the right time to find water and food.

Note: Before commencing the garment it is essential to check your tension (see below).

To Fit		S	M	L
	CM	76–81	86–91	97–102
Bust/Chest	INS	30–32	34–36	38–40
Actual	CM	106	116	127
Measurement	INS	42	46	50
Length to Back	CM	64	65	66
Neck (approx)	INS	25	25½	26
Sleeve Seam				
Women (approx)	CM	43	43	43
	INS	17	17	17
Men (approx)	CM	48	48	48
	INS	19	19	19

Note: This is a loose-fitting garment.

Materials

Cleckheaton 8 Ply Machine Wash 50 g (2 oz) balls or equivalent yarn to give stated tension.

	S	M	L
MC (Navy)	12	13	14
C (Taupe)	3	3	3

Note: You may require an extra ball of MC for men's sizes.

1 pair each 4 mm (No. 8) and 3.25 mm (No. 10) knitting needles, or **the required size to give correct tension;** 1 stitch holder; bobbins; 8 buttons.

Tension

This garment has been designed at a tension of 22 sts to 10 cm (4 ins) over st st, using 4 mm (No. 8) needles.

Note: When working from Graph A for Front, read odd numbered rows (knit rows) from right to left, and even numbered rows (purl rows) from left to right. When working from Graph A for Back, read odd numbered rows (knit rows) from left to right, and even numbered rows (purl rows) from right to left. One square represents 1 stitch.

Back

Using 3.25 mm (No. 10) needles and MC, cast on 105 (115, 127) sts.
1st Row: K2, *P1, K1, rep from * to last st, K1.
2nd Row: K1, *P1, K1, rep from * to end.
Rep 1st and 2nd rows until band measures 6 cm (2½ ins) from beg, ending with a 2nd row and inc 13 sts evenly across last row. 118 (128, 140) sts.
Change to 4 mm (No. 8) needles. Work rows 1 to 174 (176, 178) inclusive from Graph A.

Shape shoulders

Keeping Graph A correct, cast off 10 (11, 13) sts at beg of next 6 rows, then 11 (12, 11) sts at beg of foll 2 rows. Leave rem 36 (38, 40) sts on a stitch holder.

Left front

Using 3.25 mm (No. 10) needles and MC, cast on 53 (59, 65) sts. Work in rib as for lower band of Back, until band measures 6 cm (2½ ins) from beg, ending with a 2nd row and inc 6 (5, 5) sts evenly across last row. 59 (64, 70) sts.
Change to 4 mm (No. 8) needles. Work rows 1 to 157 inclusive from Graph A, as indicated for Left Front.

Shape neck

Keeping Graph A correct, cast off 9 sts at beg of next row. Dec 1 st at neck edge in 2nd row, then in **every** row until 41 (45, 50) sts rem. Work 6 (7, 8) rows.

Shape shoulder

Keeping Graph A correct, cast off 10 (11, 13) sts at beg of next and foll alt rows 3 times in all. Work 1 row. Cast off.

Right front

Work to correspond with Left Front, following Graph A as indicated for Right Front.

Sleeves

Using 3.25 mm (No. 10) needles and MC, cast on 45 (47, 49) sts. Work in rib as for

lower band of Back until band measures 6 cm (2½ ins) from beg, ending with a 2nd row and inc 15 sts evenly across last row. 60 (62, 64) sts.
Change to 4 mm (No. 8) needles. Cont in st st (1 row K, 1 row P), inc 1 st at each end of 3rd row and foll 4th rows until there are 70 (72, 74) sts. Work 3 rows. Work rows 1 to 70 inclusive from Graph B, inc 1 st at each end of next and foll 4th rows until there are 86 (94, 102) sts, then in foll 6th rows until there are 98 (102, 106) sts. Using MC, cont in st st, inc 1 st at each end of next and foll 6th row. 102 (106, 110) sts. Cont without shaping until side edge measures 43 cm (17 ins) for **Women**, or 48 cm (19 ins) for **Men**, ending with a purl row.

Shape top

Cast off 10 sts at beg of next 8 rows. Cast off rem sts.

Larripuka

Graph B

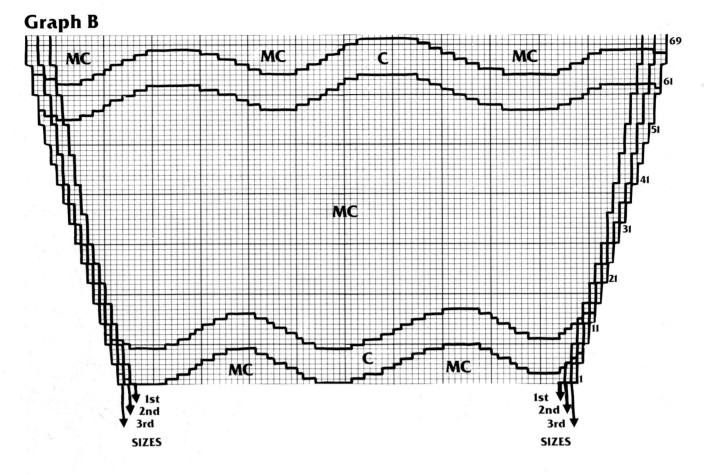

Buttonhole bands

Right front band for women, left front band for men

Using 3.25 mm (No. 10) needles and MC, cast on 11 sts.
1st Row: K2, (P1, K1) 4 times, K1.
2nd Row: (K1, P1) 5 times, K1.
3rd Row: Rib 5, cast off 2 sts, rib 4.
4th Row: Rib 4, cast on 2 sts, rib 5.
Work 24 rows rib. Rep last 26 rows 5 times, then 3rd and 4th rows once. 7 buttonholes. Work 22 rows rib. * *
Break off yarn, leave sts on a spare needle.

Left front band for women, right front band for men

Work as for other Front Band omitting buttonholes to * *. Do not break off yarn. Leave sts on needle.

Neckband

Using back-stitch, join shoulder seams. With right side facing, using 3.25 mm (No. 10) needles and MC, rib across 11 sts on Right Front Band, knit up 91 (99, 103) sts evenly around neck edge, including sts from back neck stitch holder, then rib

across Left Front Band sts. 113 (121, 125) sts. Work 7 rows rib as for lower band of Back, beg with a 2nd row of rib and working a buttonhole (as before) in 2nd and 3rd rows of Neckband. Cast off **loosely** in rib.

To make up

Using back-stitch, sew in Sleeves placing centre top of Sleeve to shoulder seam. Join side and Sleeve seams. Sew Front Bands in position stretching slightly to fit. Sew on buttons.

Larripuka

Graph A

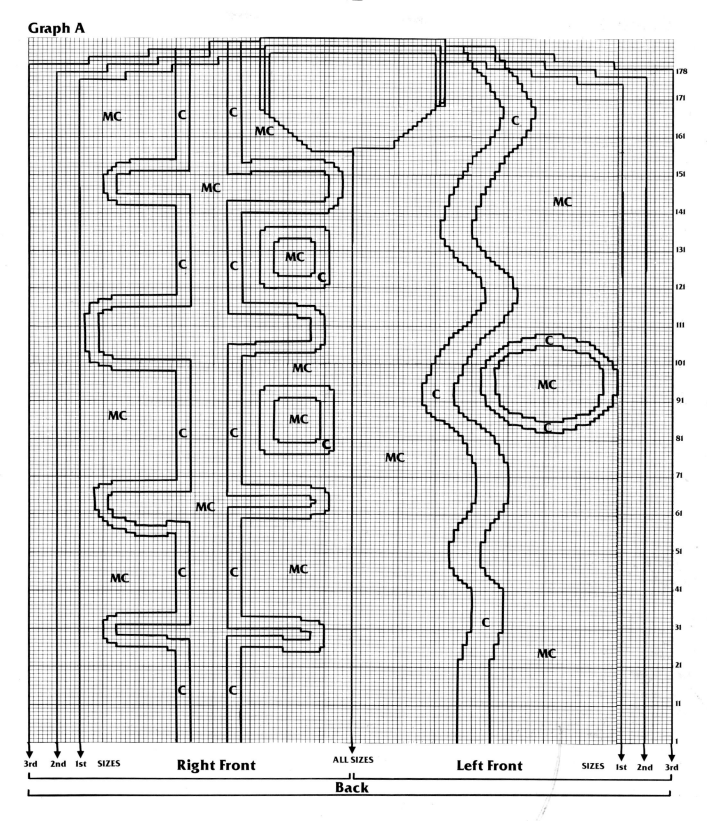

Country

Country

'By the end of the dry season about October, all the waterholes have dried up. The animals all live underground to escape the burning heat of the day. The sandhills become vary bare. Eventually the heat gives way to tropical thunderstorms. The rains begin to break and the rock holes fill with water. The country starts to come green again.'

Sandhills about five metres high roll in parallel lines across the Great Sandy Desert, and after a heavy rain they can bloom with flowers. For the designer they provide an excellent motif, parallel lines as if viewed from above, a natural patterning which also finds its way into body-painting for ceremony and the carving of designs into wood.

Note: Before commencing the garment it is essential to check your tension (see below).

		S	M	L
To Fit	CM	76-81	86-91	97-102
Bust/Chest	INS	30-32	34-36	38-40
Actual	CM	106	116	127
Measurement	INS	42	46	50
Length to Back	CM	64	65	66
Neck (approx)	INS	25	25½	26
Sleeve Seam				
Women (approx)	CM	43	43	43
	INS	17	17	17
Men (approx)	CM	48	48	48
	INS	19	19	19

Note: This is a loose-fitting garment.

Materials

Cleckheaton 8 Ply Machine Wash 50 g (2 oz) balls **or equivalent yarn to give stated tension.**

	S	M	L
MC (Jade)	6	6	7
C1 (Green)	3	3	3
C2 (Pink)	2	2	2
C4 (Brown)	2	2	2
C5 (Yellow)	1	1	1

AND **Cleckheaton The Boutique Collection Merino 8 Ply** 50 g (2 oz) balls **or equivalent yarn to give stated tension.**

C3 (Cerise)	2	2	2

Note: You may require an extra ball of MC for men's sizes.
1 pair each 4 mm (No. 8) and 3.25 mm (No. 10) knitting needles, or **the required size**

to give correct tension; 1 stitch holder; 8 buttons; bobbins.

Note: Merino 8 Ply is not machine washable.

Tension

This garment has been designed at a tension of 22 sts to 10 cm (4 ins) over st st, using 4 mm (No. 8) needles.

Back

Using 3.25 mm (No. 10) needles and C2, cast on 55 (60, 66) sts, then using MC cast on 54 (59, 65) sts.
Keeping colours correct throughout band, proceed as follows:
1st Row: K2, *P1, K1, rep from * to last st, K1.
2nd Row: K1, *P1, K1, rep from * to end.
Rep 1st and 2nd rows until band measures 8 cm (3 ins) from beg, ending with a 2nd row and inc 5 sts in C2, and 5 sts in MC evenly across last row. 119 (129, 141) sts.
Change to 4 mm (No. 8) needles and beg patt. Work rows 1 to 160 (162, 166) inclusive from Graph.

Shape shoulders

Keeping Graph correct, cast off 11 (12, 13) sts at beg of next 4 (4, 6) rows, then 10 (11, 12) sts at beg of foll 4 (4, 2) rows. Leave rem 35 (37, 39) sts on a stitch holder.

Left front

Using 3.25 mm (No. 10) needles and MC, cast on 55 (61, 67) sts. Work in rib as for lower band of Back until band measures 8 cm (3 ins) from beg, ending with a 2nd row, and inc 4 (3, 3) sts evenly across last row. 59 (64, 70) sts.
Change to 4 mm (No. 8) needles and beg patt. Work rows 1 to 143 (143, 145) inclusive from Graph as indicated for Left Front.

Shape neck

Keeping Graph correct, cast off 11 (11, 12) sts at beg of next row. Dec 1 st at neck edge in next and foll alt rows 6 (7, 7) times in all. 42 (46, 51) sts. Work 5 (5, 7) rows.

Shape shoulder

Cast off 11 (12, 13) sts at beg of next row and foll alt row, then 10 (11, 13) sts at beg of foll alt row. Work 1 row. Cast off.

Right front

Work to correspond with Left Front, following Graph for Right Front, and using C2 instead of MC for lower band.

Sleeves

Using 3.25 mm (No. 10) needles and MC, cast on 45 (47, 49) sts.
Work in rib as for lower band of Back until band measures 6 cm (2½ ins) from beg for **Women** or 7 cm (2¾ ins) from beg for **Men**, ending with a 2nd row and inc 12 sts

evenly across last row. 57 (59, 61) sts.
Change to 4 mm (No. 8) needles and beg patt. Cont in st st (1 row K, 1 row P) in stripes of 12 rows MC, 12 rows C2, 12 rows C3, 12 rows C4, 12 rows C2, 12 rows C5, 12 rows C3, 12 rows MC, and 5 rows C4, **at same time** inc 1 st at each end of 5th and foll 4th rows until there are 95 (103, 111) sts, **1st and 2nd Sizes Only —** cont inc in foll 6th rows until there are 103 (107) sts. Work 7 rows C4 (beg with a purl row), then 2 rows C2 for **Women**, or 12 rows C2 for **Men**. Work 2 rows C3 for **Men**.

Shape top

Using C2 for **Women**, or C3 for **Men**, cast off 10 sts at beg of next 8 rows. Cast off rem sts.

Buttonhole bands

Right front band for women, left front band for men

Using 3.25 mm (No. 10) needles and C2 for **Women** or MC for **Men**, cast on 11 sts. Work 4 rows rib as for lower band of Back.
5th Row: Rib 5, yfwd, K2tog, rib 4.
Work 19 rows rib. Using MC for **Women** or C2 for **Men**, knit 1 row. Work 3 rows rib.
29th Row: As 5th row.
Work 23 rows rib. Rep last 24 rows once, then first 12 of these 24 rows once. Using C5, knit 1 row. Work 7 rows rib. Using MC, knit 1 row. Work 3 rows rib.
101st Row: As 5th row.
Work 1 row rib. Using C1, knit 1 row. Work 21 rows rib.
125th Row: As 5th row.
Work 23 rows rib.
149th Row: As 5th row.
Work 19 rows rib. 7 buttonholes. Leave sts on a spare needle.

Left front band for women, right front band for men

Work as for other Front Band omitting

Country

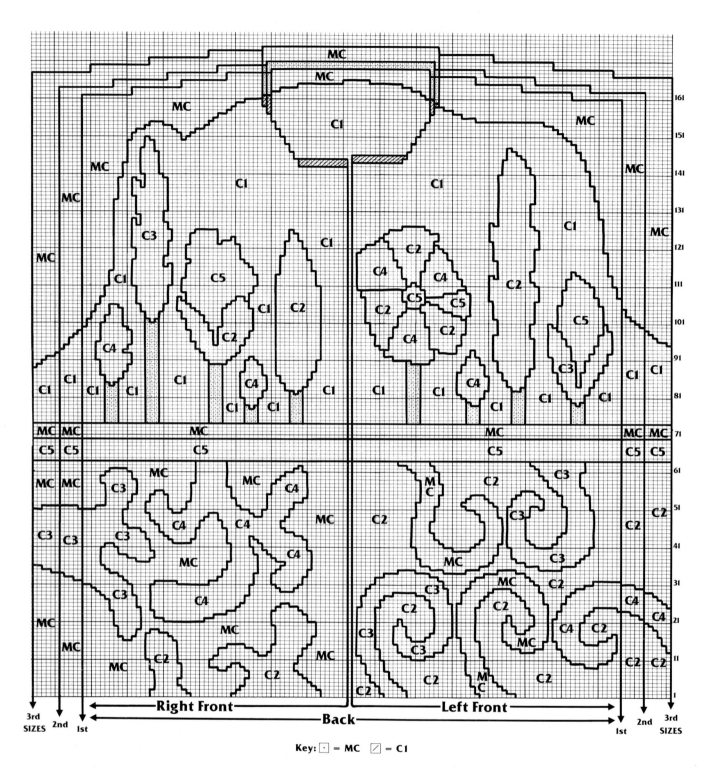

Key: ⊡ = MC ⊘ = C1

buttonholes and using MC in place of C2, and C2 in place of MC in first 88 rows.

Neckband

Using back-stitch, join shoulder seams. With right side facing, using 3.25 mm (No. 10) needles and C1, rib across Right Front Band sts, knit up 89 (95, 103) sts evenly around neck edge, including sts

from stitch holder changing to MC to match colour on body of jumper, then rib across Left Front Band sts. 111 (117, 125) sts. Work 3 rows rib.

Women: 4th Row Rib 4, yfwd, K2tog, rib to end.

Men: 4th Row Rib to last 5 sts, yfwd, K2tog, rib 3.

All sizes work 3 rows rib. Cast off **loosely** in rib.

To make up

Using back-stitch, sew in Sleeves placing centre top of Sleeve to shoulder seam. Join side and Sleeve seams. Sew Front Bands in position stretching slightly to fit. Sew on buttons.

Mangkaja - White Bird

Mangkaja - White Bird

'Mangkaja *or* Wiringarri *is a white bird from the Dreamtime. He is like an owl, with black and white markings around his eyes. He travels at night.* Mangkaja *come from the place called* Kiyili. *Some people were frightened of this* Mangkaja. *They found him sitting down on a log. They tried to kill him, but he flew up very high, and where he landed there sprung up a waterhole,* Magkajakura.

'When he comes down, he sinks down and the ground sinks down. As he goes down, he goes round in a circle, and makes steps in the rock right round. People can climb down the steps when they get water.

'This is* Jilji [*sandhill*] *country.*

'Mangkaja *comes at night, you can hear him making a noise — like* tchya tchya, *underneath the water.*

'Nearby this place is* Malajapi, *the campsite of the* Mala *spirit.* Mala *is the little bush kangaroo. The people came here to tell the spirit to send plenty of* Mala *to the land.'*

This Dreaming story is of the kind that talks about spirits and other frightening things that are only scarcely visible to ordinary people. It is also a story about increase, calling on the spirit to bring plenty of kangaroos to the country, perhaps to the waterhole connected with this 'owl' from the Dreaming.

Note: Before commencing the garment it is essential to check your tension (see below).

		S	M	L
To Fit	CM	76–81	86–91	97–102
Bust/Chest	INS	30–32	34–36	38–40
Actual	CM	106	116	127
Measurement	INS	42	46	50
Length to Back	CM	64	65	66
Neck (approx)	INS	25	25½	26
Sleeve Seam				
Women (approx)	CM	43	43	43
	INS	17	17	17
Men (approx)	CM	48	48	48
	INS	19	19	19

Note: This is a loose-fitting garment.

Materials

Cleckheaton 8 Ply Machine Wash 50 g (2 oz) balls **or equivalent yarn to give stated tension.**

	S	M	L
MC (Black)	12	13	14
C (White)	2	2	2

Note: You may require an extra ball of MC for men's sizes.
1 pair each 4 mm (No. 8) and 3.25 mm (No. 10), and 1 set of 3.25 mm (No. 10) knitting needles, or **the required size to give correct tension;**
2 stitch holders; bobbins.

Tension

This garment has been designed at a tension of 22 sts to 10 cm (4 ins) over st st, using 4 mm (No. 8) needles.

Front

Using 3.25 mm (No. 10) needles and MC, cast on 103 (113, 125) sts.
1st Row: K2, *P1, K1, rep from * to last st, K1.
2nd Row: K1, *P1, K1, rep from * to end.
Rep 1st and 2nd rows until band measures 8 cm (3 ins) from beg, ending with a 2nd row and inc 16 sts evenly across last row. 119 (129, 141) sts.
Change to 4 mm (No. 8) needles and beg patt. **Work rows 1 to 142 (142, 144) inclusive from Graph.

Shape neck

Keeping Graph correct,
Next Row: K48 (53, 58), **turn.** Dec 1 st at left neck edge in alt rows 6 (7, 7) times. 42 (46, 51) sts. Work 5 (5, 7) rows.

Shape shoulder

Cast off 11 (12, 13) sts at beg of next row and foll alt row, then 10 (11, 13) sts at beg of foll alt row. Work 1 row. Cast off. Slip next 23 (23, 25) sts onto a stitch holder and leave. Join yarn to rem sts and complete right hand side of neck to correspond with left side.

Back

Work as for Front to **. Cont in st st (1 row K, 1 row P) until Back measures same as Front to shoulder shaping, ending with a purl row.

Shape shoulders

Cast off 11 (12, 13) sts at beg of next 4 (4, 6) rows, then 10 (11, 12) sts at beg of foll 4 (4, 2) rows. Leave rem 35 (37, 39) sts on a stitch holder.

Sleeves

Using 3.25 mm (No. 10) needles and MC, cast on 43 (45, 47) sts. Work in rib as for lower band of Front until band measures 8 cm (3 ins) from beg, ending with a 2nd row and inc 14 sts evenly across last row. 57 (59, 61) sts.

Change to 4 mm (No. 8) needles. Cont in st st inc 1 st at each end of 5th and foll 4th rows until there are 95 (103, 111) sts, **1st and 2nd Sizes Only** — then in foll 6th rows until there are 103 (107, 111) sts. Cont without shaping until side edge measures 43 cm for **Women** or 48 cm for **Men**, ending with a purl row.

Shape top

Cast off 10 sts at beg of next 8 rows.
Cast off rem sts.

Neckband

Using back-stitch, join shoulder seams. With right side facing, using set of 3.25 mm (No. 10) needles and MC, knit up 98 (104, 112) sts evenly around neck edge, including sts from stitch holders.
1st Round: *K1, P1, rep from * to end. Rep 1st round 9 times. Cast off **loosely** in rib.

To make up

Using back-stitch, sew in Sleeves placing centre top of Sleeve to shoulder seam. Join side and Sleeve seams.

Mangkaja - White Bird

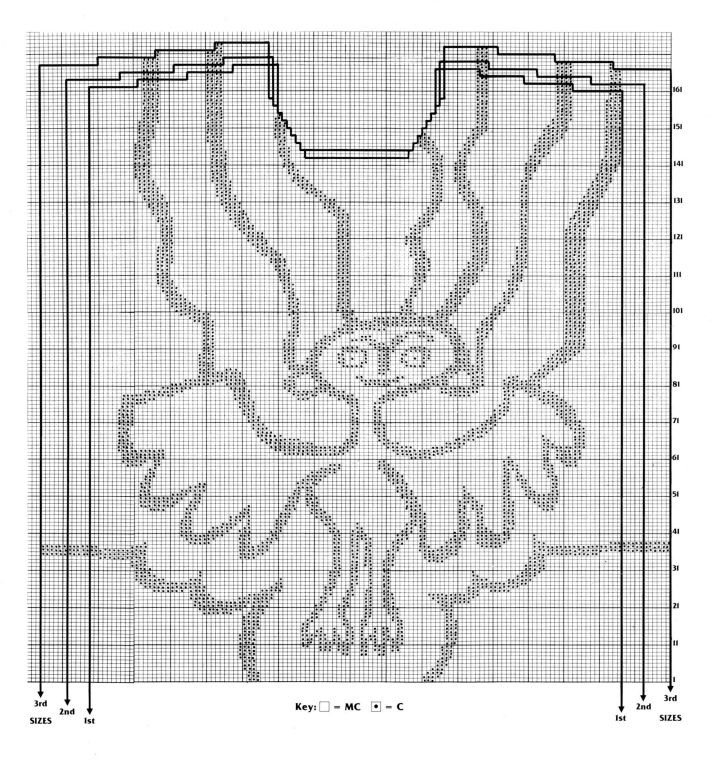

Key: ☐ = MC ⊡ = C

3rd SIZES 2nd 1st

1st 2nd 3rd SIZES

Partiri - Desert Flowers

Partiri - Desert Flowers

'The trees all change in the rainy season. They are covered with new growth and flowers. The grass grows long. Desert flowers start to come up in the hollows between sandhills, turning all colours. These are called partiri *in the local Aboriginal language.'*

Regrowth after rain can produce an abundance of bush fruits, including bush plum, bush banana, tomato, and blossoms that can be sucked for their honey. These fruits are often quite small, but they are rich in vitamins and minerals and provide a valuable supplement to a diet of meat, various sorts of yam, grubs and ground seeds.

Note: Before commencing the garment it is essential to check your tension (see below).

		S	M	L
To Fit	CM	76-81	86-91	97-102
Bust/Chest	INS	30-32	34-36	38-40
Actual	CM	106	116	127
Measurement	INS	42	46	50
Length to	CM	64	65	66
Back Neck	INS	25	25½	26
Sleeve Seam				
Women	CM	43	43	43
	INS	17	17	17
Men	CM	48	48	48
	INS	19	19	19

Note: This is a loose-fitting garment.

Materials

Cleckheaton 8 Ply Machine Wash 50 g (2 oz) balls **or equivalent yarn to give stated tension.**

	S	M	L
MC (Green)	4	5	6
C1 (Rust)	4	4	4
C2 (Navy)	2	3	3
C3 (Aqua)	2	2	2
C4 (Yellow)	1	1	1
C5 (Carrot)	1	1	1
C6 (Bottle Green)	1	1	1
C7 (Pink)	1	1	1
C8 (Red)	1	1	1

Note: You may require an extra ball of MC for men's sizes.
1 pair each 4 mm (No. 8) and 3.25 mm (No. 10), and 1 set of 3.25 mm (No. 10) knitting needles, or **the required size to give correct tension**, 2 stitch holders; bobbins.

Tension

This garment has been designed at a tension of 22 sts to 10 cm over st st, using 4 mm (No. 8) needles.

Back

Using 3.25 mm (No. 10) needles and MC, cast on 105 (115, 127) sts.
1st Row: K2, *P1, K1, rep from * to last st, K1.
2nd Row: K1, *P1, K1, rep from * to end.
Rep 1st and 2nd rows until band measures 6 cm (2½ ins) from beg, ending with a 2nd row and inc 13 sts evenly across last row. 118 (128, 140) sts.
Change to 4 mm (No. 8) needles. Work 20 rows st st (1 row K, 1 row P).** Work rows 1 to 148 inclusive from Graph A. Using C2, cont in st st until work measures 64 (65, 66) cm from beg, ending with a purl row.

Shape shoulders

Cast off 10 (11, 13) sts at beg of next 6 rows, then 11 (12, 11) sts at beg of foll 2 rows. Leave rem 36 (38, 40) sts on a stitch holder.

Front

Work as for Back to **. Work rows 1 to 136 inclusive from Graph A.

Shape neck

Next Row: K47 (52, 58), **turn**.
Keeping Graph A correct, dec 1 st at left neck edge in foll alt rows 5 times. 42 (47, 53) sts rem. Work 1 row. Using C2, cont in st st, dec 1 st at neck edge in next row, **2nd and 3rd Sizes Only** — cont dec in foll alt row/s until (45, 50) sts rem. 41 (45, 50) sts. Cont in st st until work measures 64 (65, 66) cm from beg, ending with a purl row.

Shape shoulder

Cast off 10 (11, 13) sts at beg of next and foll alt rows 3 times in all. Work 1 row. Cast off. Slip next 24 sts onto a stitch holder and leave. Join yarn to rem sts at right neck edge and complete to correspond with left side.

Sleeves

Using 3.25 mm (No. 10) needles and MC, cast on 45 (47, 49) sts. Work in rib as for lower band of Back until band measures 6 cm (2½ ins) from beg, ending with a 2nd row and inc 15 sts evenly across last row. 60 (62, 64) sts.
Change to 4 mm (No. 8) needles. Cont in st st, inc 1 st at each end of 3rd row. 62 (64, 66) sts. Work 1 row. Work rows 1 to 106 inclusive from Graph B inc 1 st at each end of 3rd and foll 4th rows until there are 86 (94, 102) sts, then in foll 6th rows until there are 102 (106, 110) sts. Rep last 2 rows until side edge measures 43 cm (17 ins) for **Women** or 48 cm (19 ins) for **Men** ending with a purl row.

Shape top

Keeping placement of colours in last 2 rows correct, cast off 10 sts at beg of next 8 rows. Cast off rem sts.

Neckband

Using back-stitch, join shoulder seams. With right side facing, using set of 3.25 mm (No. 10) needles, beg at left shoulder seam, knit up 96 (102, 108) sts evenly around neck edge including sts from stitch holders, matching colours in Neckband to body of Jumper.
1st Round: *K1, P1, rep from * to end. Rep 1st round until neckband measures 5 cm (2 ins) from beg. Cast off **loosely** in rib.

To make up

Using back-stitch, sew in Sleeves placing centre top of Sleeve to shoulder seam. Join side and Sleeve seams. Fold Neckband in half onto wrong side and slip-stitch in position.

Partiri - Desert Flowers

Graph A

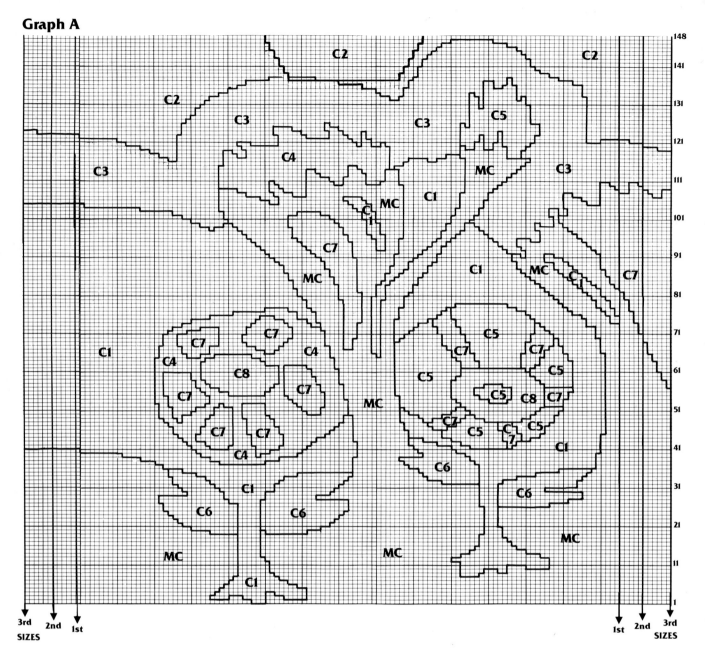

Partiri - Desert Flowers

Graph B

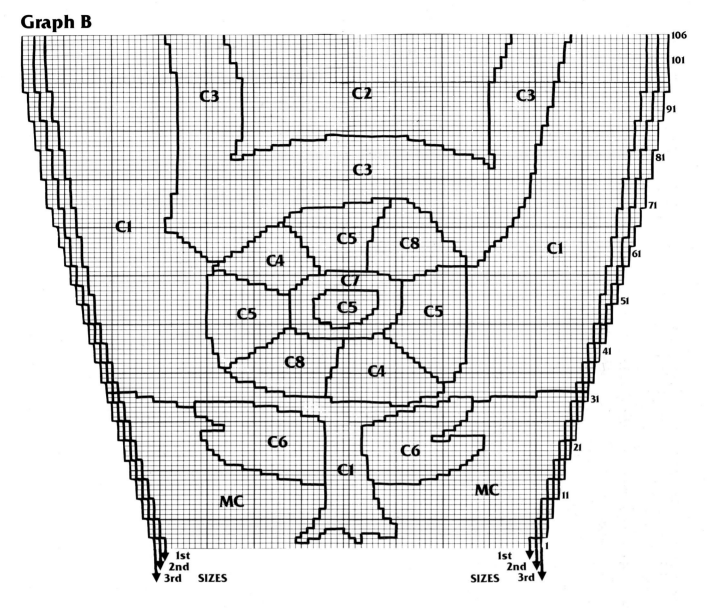

Two Little Girls

Two Little Girls

'One mother had two baby girls, at one waterhole. Two girls find butterfly flying towards them. They try to grab them. They miss them. They chase them all the way. They come up to a big mob of women, who pick up the two girls. The mother came back and find them gone. She follow their tracks and come to the women and asked for her two girls, but they wouldn't give her back the two babies.'

This is a cautionary tale for children, with the moral that they shouldn't stray too far into the bush. Stories like this are told to children around the camp-fire. While this story has its basis in an actual event, it is of general relevance to Aboriginal society and the need to discipline children. There are never many children in the traditional desert-dwelling society which practised birth control because of scarce resources. This perhaps explains why the other women were not willing to give up the girls, the producers of future generations.

Note: Before commencing the garment it is essential to check your tension (see below).

		S	M	L
To Fit	CM	76-81	86-91	97-102
Bust/Chest	INS	30-32	34-36	38-40
Actual	CM	106	116	127
Measurement	INS	42	46	50
Length to Back	CM	70	71	72
Neck (approx)	INS	27½	28	28½
Sleeve Seam				
Women (approx)	CM	43	43	43
	INS	17	17	17
Men (approx)	CM	48	48	48
	INS	19	19	19

Note: This is a loose-fitting garment.

Materials

Cleckheaton Natural 8 Ply 50 g (2 oz) balls or equivalent yarn to give stated tension.

	S	M	L
MC (Black)	14	15	16
C (White)	2	2	2

Note: You may require an extra ball of MC, for men's sizes.

1 pair each 4 mm (No. 8) and 3.25 mm (No. 10), and 1 set of 3.25 mm (No. 10) knitting needles, or **the required size to give correct tension**; 2 stitch holders; bobbins.

Tension

This garment has been designed at a tension of 22 sts to 10 cm (4 ins) over st st, using 4 mm (No. 8) needles.

Front

Using 3.25 mm (No. 10) needles and MC, cast on 105 (115, 127) sts.
1st Row: K2, *P1, K1, rep from * to last st, K1.
2nd Row: K1, *P1, K1, rep from * to end.
Rep 1st and 2nd rows until band measures 6 cm (2½ ins) from beg, ending with a 2nd row and inc 13 sts evenly across last row. 118 (128, 140) sts.
Change to 4 mm (No. 8) needles. ** Work rows 1 to 156 inclusive from Graph A.

Shape neck

Next Row: Keeping Graph correct, 47 (52, 58), **turn**.
Keeping Graph A correct, dec 1 st at left neck edge in alt rows 6 (7, 8) times. 41 (45, 50) sts rem. Work 5 rows.

Shape shoulder

Keeping Graph A correct, cast off 10 (11, 13) sts at beg of next and foll alt rows 3 times in all. Work 1 row. Cast off. Slip next 24 sts onto a stitch holder and leave. Join yarn to rem sts at right neck edge and complete to correspond with left side of neck.

Back

Work as for Front to **. Using MC, cont in st st (1 row K, 1 row P) until work measures same as Front to shoulder shaping.

Shape shoulders

Cast off 10 (11, 13) sts at beg of next 6 rows, then 11 (12, 11) sts at beg of foll 2 rows. Leave rem 36 (38, 40) sts on a stitch holder.

Right sleeve

Using 3.25 mm (No. 10) needles and MC, cast on 45 (47, 49) sts. Work in rib as for lower band of Back until band measures 6 cm (2½ ins) from beg, ending with a 2nd row and inc 15 sts evenly across last row. 60 (62, 64) sts.
Change to 4 mm (No. 8) needles. *** Cont in st st, inc 1 st at each end of 3rd row and foll 4th rows until there are 80 (82, 84) sts. Work 3 rows.
Work rows 1 to 46 inclusive from Graph B, **at same time** inc 1 st at each end of next and foll 4th rows until there are 86 (94, 102) sts, then in foll 6th rows until there are 98 (102, 106) sts. Using MC, cont in st st, inc 1 st at each end of 5th row and foll 6th row. 102 (106, 110) sts. Cont without

shaping until side edge measures 43 cm (17 ins) for **Women** and 48 cm (19 ins) for **Men**, ending with a purl row.

Shape top

Cast off 10 sts at beg of next 8 rows. Cast off rem sts.

Left sleeve

Work as for Right Sleeve to ***. Cont in st st, inc 1 st at each end of 3rd row and foll 4th rows until there are 86 (92, 94) sts, **1st Size Only** — then in foll 6th row once. Work 2 (0, 0) rows. Work rows 1 to 41 inclusive from Graph C (beg with a purl row), **at same time** inc 1 st at each end of 4th row and foll 6th (6th, 4th) rows until there are 102 (106, 102) sts, **3rd Size Only** — cont inc in foll 6th rows until there are 110 sts.
Using MC, cont in st st without shaping until side edge measures 43 cm (17 ins) for **Women** and 48 cm (19 ins) for **Men**, ending with a purl row.

Shape top

Complete as for Right Sleeve.

Neckband

Using back-stitch, join shoulder seams. With right side facing, using set of 3.25 mm (No. 10) needles and MC, beg at left shoulder seam, knit up 96 (102, 108) sts evenly around neck edge, including sts from stitch holders.
1st Round: *K1, P1, rep from * to end. Rep 1st round until neckband measures 5 cm (2 ins) from beg. Cast off **loosely** in rib.

To make up

Using back-stitch, sew in Sleeves placing centre top of Sleeve to shoulder seam. Join side and Sleeve seams. Fold Neckband in half onto wrong side and slip-stitch in position.

Two Little Girls

Graph A

176
171
161
151
141
131
121
111
101
91
81
71
61
51
41
31
21
11
1

3rd 2nd 1st SIZES

Key: ☐ = MC ⊡ = C

SIZES 1st 2nd 3rd

Two Little Girls

Graph B

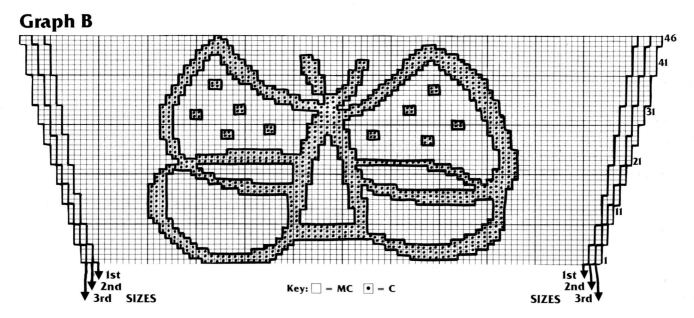

Graph C

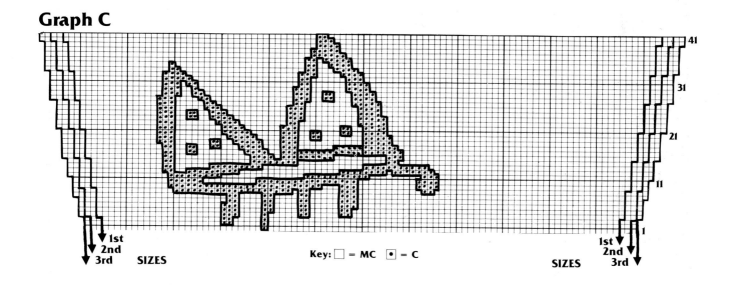

Flowers After the Rain

Flowers After the Rain

'*After the rainy season is the time for flowers. All the different trees change in the winter time. They get flowers and new growth. Grass and flowers grow in the flat country in between the sandhills. The flowers turn all colours, purple, pink and blue. They grow in all the bush, not just near waterholes.*'

There are five seasons in northern Australia, and the rainy season is a crucial one. At times during 'the wet', there can be heavy rainfall and tropical monsoons can cause flooding, even in the desert areas. After the wet, grass and flowers which have lain dormant burst into life.

Note: Before commencing the garment it is essential to check your tension (see below).

		S	M	L
To Fit	CM	76–81	86–91	97–102
Bust/Chest	INS	30–32	34–36	38–40
Actual	CM	106	116	127
Measurement	INS	42	46	50
Length to	CM	65	66	67
Back Neck	INS	25½	26	26½
Sleeve Seam				
Women (approx)	CM	43	43	43
	INS	17	17	17
Men (approx)	CM	48	48	48
	INS	19	19	19

Note: This is a loose-fitting garment.

Materials

Cleckheaton 8 Ply Machine Wash 50 g (2 oz) balls **or equivalent yarn to give stated tension.**

	S	M	L
MC (Grey)	12	13	14
C1 (Black)	2	2	2
C2 (White)	1	1	1
C3 (Aqua)	1	1	1
C4 (Mauve)	1	1	1

Note: You may require an extra ball of MC for men's sizes.
1 pair each 4 mm (No. 8) and 3.25 mm (No. 10), and 1 set of 3.25 mm (No. 10) knitting needles, or **the required size to give correct tension**; 2 stitch holders; bobbins.

Tension

This garment has been designed at a tension of 22 sts to 10 cm (4 ins) over st st, using 4 mm (No. 8) needles.

Back

Using 3.25 mm (No. 10) needles and MC, cast on 105 (115, 127) sts.
1st Row: K2, *P1, K1, rep from * to last st, K1.
2nd Row: K1, *P1, K1, rep from * to end.
Rep 1st and 2nd rows until band measures 6 cm (2½ ins) from beg, ending with a 2nd row and inc 13 sts evenly across last row. 118 (128, 140) sts.
Change to 4 mm (No. 8) needles. * * Work rows 1 to 162 inclusive from Graph A. Using MC, cont in st st (1 row K, 1 row P) until work measures 64 (65, 66) cm (25 [25½, 26] ins) from beg, ending with a purl row.

Shape shoulders

Cast off 10 (11, 13) sts at beg of next 6 rows, then 11 (12, 11) sts at beg of foll 2 rows. Leave rem 36 (38, 40) sts on a stitch holder.

Front

Work as for Back to * *. Work rows 1 to 156 inclusive from Graph A.

Shape neck

Keeping Graph A correct,
Next Row: K47 (52, 58), **turn**.
Dec 1 st at left neck edge in foll alt rows twice. 45 (50, 56) sts rem. Work 1 row. Using MC, cont in st st, dec 1 st at neck edge in next and foll alt rows until 41(45, 50) sts rem. Cont without shaping until work measures 64 (65, 66) cm (25 [25½, 26] ins) from beg, ending with a purl row.

Shape shoulder

Cast off 10 (11, 13) sts at beg of next and foll alt rows 3 times in all. Work 1 row. Cast off. Slip next 24 sts onto a stitch holder and leave. Join yarn to rem sts at right neck edge and complete to correspond with left side of neck.

Sleeves

Using 3.25 mm (No. 10) needles and MC, cast on 45 (47, 49) sts.
Work in rib as for lower band of Back, until band measures 6 cm (2½ ins) from beg, ending with a 2nd row and inc 15 sts evenly across last row. 60 (62, 64) sts.
Change to 4 mm (No. 8) needles. Cont in st st, inc 1 st at each end of 3rd and foll 4th rows until there are 74 (76, 78) sts. Work 1 row. Work rows 1 to 68 inclusive from Graph B, at the same time, inc 1 st at each end of 3rd and foll 4th rows until there are 86 (94, 102) sts, then in foll 6th rows until there are 100 (104, 108) sts.
Using MC, cont in st st, inc 1 st at each end of 3rd row. 102 (106, 110) sts.
Cont without shaping until side edge measures 43 cm (17 ins) for **Women** or 48 cm (19 ins) for **Men**, ending with a purl row.

Shape top

Cast off 10 sts at beg of next 8 rows. Cast off rem sts.

Neckband

Using back-stitch, join shoulder seams. With right side facing, using set of 3.25 mm (No. 10) needles and MC, beg at left shoulder seam, knit up 96 (102, 108) sts evenly around neck edge, including sts from stitch holders.
1st Round: *K1, P1, rep from * to end. Rep 1st round until Neckband measures 5 cm (2 ins) from beg. Cast off **loosely** in rib.

To make up

Using back-stitch, sew in Sleeves placing centre top of Sleeve to shoulder seam. Join side and Sleeve seams. Fold Neckband in half onto wrong side and slip-stitch in position.

Flowers After the Rain

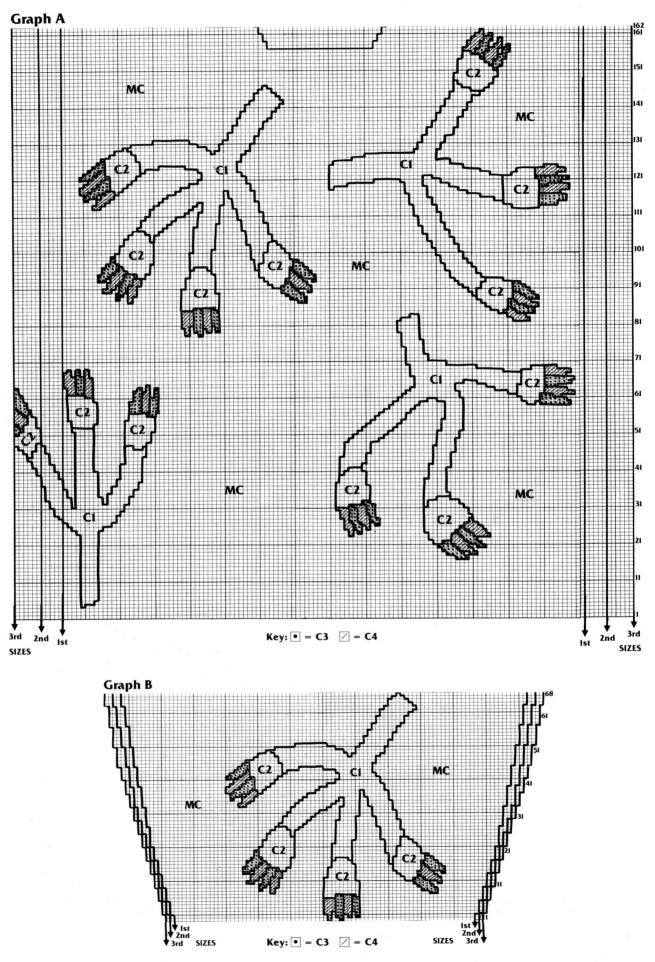

Graph A

Graph B

Key: • = C3   ⁄ = C4

Kartiya Boat

Kartiya Boat

'When the first kartiya came to Australia with a boat; when they first find Australia. That's a reef and land; he's coming into that land.'

In Jimmy Pike's country, Europeans are called *kartiya*. This design was commissioned for a poster during the 1988 bicentennial celebrations, and it illustrates an Aboriginal perception of colonisation. The design is a perfect example of the way Jimmy Pike can combine Western art with his own. The image is that of a boat clearly enough, but it also incorporates the interlocking lines and colours of Pike's culture from the Great Sandy Desert.

Note: Before commencing the garment it is essential to check your tension (see below).

		S	M	L
To Fit	CM	76-81	86-91	97-102
Bust/Chest	INS	30-32	34-36	38-40
Actual	CM	106	116	127
Measurement	INS	42	46	50
Length to	CM	64	65	66
Back Neck	INS	25	25½	26
Sleeve Seam				
Women	CM	43	43	43
	INS	17	17	17
Men	CM	48	48	48
	INS	19	19	19

Note: This is a loose-fitting garment.

Materials

Cleckheaton 8 Ply Machine Wash 50 g (2 oz) balls **or equivalent yarn to give stated tension.**

	S	M	L
MC (Aqua)	10	11	12
C1 (Cobalt)	3	3	3

1 ball each of 6 contrasting colours (C2-Green, C3-Yellow, C4-Purple, C5-Red, C6-Rust, C7-Black).

Note: You may require an extra ball of MC for men's sizes.

1 pair each 4 mm (No. 8) and 3.25 mm (No. 10), and 1 set of 3.25 mm (No. 10) knitting needles, or **the required size to give correct tension**; 2 stitch holders; bobbins.

Tension

This garment has been designed at a tension of 22 sts to 10 cm (4 ins) over st st, using 4 mm (No. 8) needles.

Back

Using 3.25 mm (No. 10) needles and C1, cast on 105 (115, 127) sts.
1st Row: K2, *P1, K1, rep from * to last st, K1.
2nd Row: K1, *P1, K1, rep from * to end.
Rep 1st and 2nd rows until band measures 6 cm (2½ ins) from beg, ending with a 2nd row and inc 13 sts evenly across last row. 118 (128, 140) sts.
Change to 4 mm (No. 8) needles. ** Work 36 (36, 34) rows st st (1 row K, 1 row P). Using MC, cont in st st until work measures 64 (65, 66) cm (25 [25½, 26] ins) from beg, ending with a purl row.

Shape shoulders

Cast off 10 (11, 13) sts at beg of next 6 rows, then 11 (12, 11) sts at beg of foll 2 rows. Leave rem 36 (38, 40) sts on a stitch holder.

Front

Work as for Back to **. Work 30 rows st st. Work rows 1 to 122 inclusive from Graph. Using MC, cont in st st until there are 18 (20, 22) rows less than Back to shoulder shaping.

Shape neck

Next Row: K47 (52, 58), **turn**.
Dec 1 st at left neck edge in alt rows 6 (7, 8) times. 41 (45, 50) sts rem. Work 5 rows.

Shape shoulder

Cast off 10 (11, 13) sts at beg of next and foll alt rows, 3 times in all. Work 1 row. Cast off. Slip next 24 sts onto a stitch holder and leave. Join yarn to rem sts at right neck edge and complete to correspond with left side.

Sleeves

Using 3.25 mm (No. 10) needles and MC, cast on 45 (47, 49) sts.
Work in rib as for lower band of Back until band measures 6 cm (2½ ins) from beg, ending with a 2nd row and inc 15 sts evenly across last row. 60 (62, 64) sts.
Change to 4 mm (No. 8) needles. Cont in st st, inc 1 st at each end of 3rd and foll 4th rows until there are 86 (94, 102) sts, then in foll 6th rows until there are 102 (106, 110) sts. Cont without shaping until side edge measures 43 cm (17 ins) for **Women** or 48 cm (19 ins) for **Men**, ending with a purl row.

Shape top

Cast off 10 sts at beg of next 8 rows. Cast off rem sts.

Neckband

Using back-stitch, join shoulder seams. With right side facing, using set of 3.25 mm (No. 10) needles and MC, beg at left shoulder seam, knit up 96 (102, 108) sts evenly around neck edge including sts from stitch holders.
1st Round: *K1, P1, rep from * to end. Rep 1st round until neckband measures 5 cm (2 ins) from beg. Cast off **loosely** in rib.

To make up

Using back-stitch, sew in Sleeves placing centre top of Sleeve to shoulder seam. Join side and Sleeve seams. Fold Neckband in half onto wrong side and slip-stitch in position.

Kartiya Boat

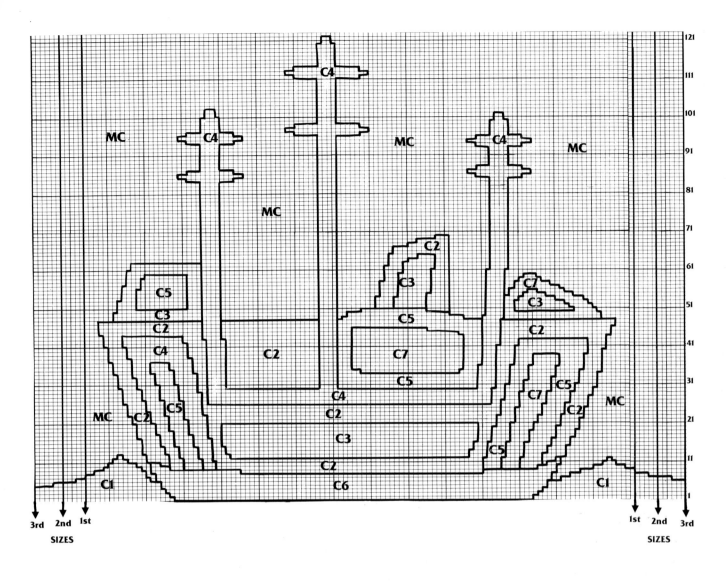

Kurntumaru and Parnaparnt

Kurntumaru and Parnaparnti

'Kurntumaru *and* Parnaparnti *are two cousin-brothers. In the Dreamtime they tracked all the snakes. They been go in a long big hole. They touched the snakes with a stick. The names of that place are* Wurrampangu *and* Narlkartuwarnti. *All the big sandhills called* Japi *are there, very dangerous to people. That's a Dreamtime place that's* Wituka *country. The two cousin-brothers went all through that country.'*

Jimmy Pike's story is from the Dreamtime. This is not a historical period, but a set of stories which are of crucial importance in the culture. It describes the relationship between human beings and natural phenomena like animals and landforms. In this design the important elements are the snake, the sandhills and the two men.

Note: Before commencing the garment it is essential to check your tension (see below).

		S	M	L
To Fit	CM	76-81	86-91	97-102
Bust/Chest	INS	30-32	34-36	38-40
Actual	CM	106	116	127
Measurement	INS	42	46	50
Length to Back	CM	64	65	66
Neck (approx)	INS	25	25½	26
Sleeve Seam				
Women (approx)	CM	43	43	43
	INS	17	17	17
Men (approx)	CM	48	48	48
	INS	19	19	19

Note: This is a loose-fitting garment.

Materials

Cleckheaton Natural 8 Ply 50 g (2 oz) balls or equivalent yarn to give stated tension.

	S	M	L
MC (Rust)	12	13	14
C1 (Brown)	2	2	2
C2 (Sand)	1	1	1
C3 (Black)	Small Quantity		

Note: You may require an extra ball of MC for men's sizes.
1 pair each 4 mm (No. 8) and 3.25 mm (No. 10), and 1 set of 3.25 mm (No. 10) knitting needles, or **the required size to give correct tension**;
2 stitch holders; bobbins.

Tension

This garment has been designed at a tension of 22 sts to 10 cm (4 ins) over st st, using 4 mm (No. 8) needles.

Front

Using 3.25 mm (No. 10) needles and MC, cast on 103 (113, 125) sts.
1st Row: K2, *P1, K1, rep from * to last st, K1.
2nd Row: K1, *P1, K1, rep from * to end.
Rep 1st and 2nd rows until band measures 8 cm (3 ins) from beg, ending with a 2nd row and inc 16 sts evenly across last row. 119 (129, 141) sts.
Change to 4 mm (No. 8) needles and beg patt.** Work rows 1 to 142 (142, 144) inclusive from Graph A.

Shape neck

Keeping Graph A correct,
Next Row: K48 (53, 58), **turn.**
Dec 1 st at left neck edge in alt rows 6 (7, 7) times. 42 (46, 51) sts. Work 5 (5, 7) rows.

Shape shoulder

Cast off 11 (12, 13) sts at beg of next row and foll alt row, then 10 (11, 13) sts at beg of foll alt row. Work 1 row. Cast off. Slip next 23 (23, 25) sts onto a stitch holder and leave. Join yarn to rem sts and complete right hand side of neck to correspond with left side.

Back

Work as for Front to **. Cont in st st (1 row K, 1 row P), using MC throughout, until Back measures same as Front to shoulder shaping, ending with a purl row.

Shape shoulders

Cast off 11 (12, 13) sts at beg of next 4 (4, 6) rows, then 10 (11, 12) sts at beg of foll 4 (4, 2) rows. Leave rem 35 (37, 39) sts on a stitch holder.

Right sleeve

Using 3.25 mm (No. 10) needles and MC, cast on 43 (45, 47) sts. Work 8 cm (3 ins) rib as for lower band of Front, ending with a 2nd row and inc 14 sts evenly across last row. 57 (59, 61) sts.
Change to 4 mm (No. 8) needles. Work rows 1 to 98 inclusive from Graph B for **Women** or rows 1 to 112 inclusive for **Men, at same time** inc 1 st at each end of 5th and foll 4th (alt, alt) rows until there are 101 (63, 69) sts, then in foll 6th (4th, 4th) row/s until there are 103 (107, 111) sts.

Shape top

Keeping Graph correct, cast off 10 sts at beg of next 8 rows. Cast off rem sts.

Left sleeve

Work as for Right Sleeve following Graph C instead of Graph B.

Neckband

Using back-stitch, join shoulder seams. With right side facing, using set of 3.25 mm (No. 10) needles and MC, knit up 92 (98, 106) sts evenly around neck edge, including sts from stitch holders.
1st Round: *K1, P1, rep from * to end.
Rep 1st round 9 times. Cast off **loosely** in rib.

To make up

Using back-stitch, sew in Sleeves placing centre top of Sleeve to shoulder seam. Join side and Sleeve seams. Using stem stitch, and black yarn, embroider eyes and mouths.

Kurntumaru and Parnaparnti

Graph A

Kurntumaru and Parnaparnti

Graph B

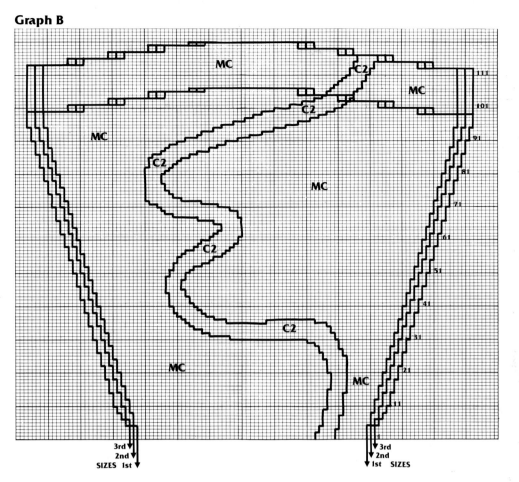

Graph C

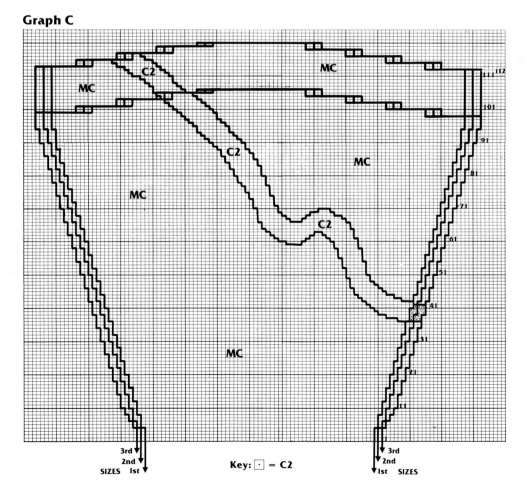

Key: ⊡ = C2

KUKAKU

DEAGGIDDITT

DEAGGIDDITT is an artist from the central southern desert region of Western Australia, where the people call themselves *Wangai* and speak the *Wangkatjaku Wangka* language. Deaggidditt was born at Leonora in 1959 and as he grew up his grandparents related to him the stories of the spirit ancestors of his people.

While his father was a traditional tribal man from the bush, Deaggidditt grew up around the goldfields in Western Australia and on remote cattle and sheep stations. When he was a child he went to a mission school for a year and later spent a year in high school in Kalgoorlie.

His first art work was done in charcoal on asbestos. Using available materials, he drew on fences, water tanks and concrete pavements. At high school in Kalgoorlie, his teacher encouraged him to develop his artistic interest, and also taught him silk-screen printing on T-shirts. After he left school he painted in his spare time, sharing his ideas with older Aboriginal artists, some of whom have never been artistically recognised. Since he was a child one of his favourite artists has been Albert Namatjira, the celebrated Aboriginal artist who worked in watercolour styles during the 1950s.

Over the past five years Deaggidditt has learnt etching and printing, spending more time on printing. He likes printing because he can use strong colours and lines, putting a lot of detail into the images. Deaggidditt has recreated the traditional stories of his childhood in his paintings and prints. He makes simple and powerful images of animals, spirits, hunting scenes and everyday events, as well as images of the stories that form part of the culture of his community. The *Wangai* have a strong graphic tradition which includes drawing stories in the sand as they are being told. While some of his work is purely for enjoyment, he is also keen to work for commercial fabric printing. Deaggidditt says: 'I have chosen these prints because they have a lot of feeling in them. They are full of laughter and joking.'

DEAGGIDDITT

Emu - Bush Food

Emu - Bush Food

'The emu is bush food for the people. When we get an emu, we got to kill it and cook it straight away. He's got like a poison bag inside, you've got to cut it out.
'First you take off all the feathers. They use feathers for dance ceremonies and to make shoes. Then they clean the carcass and throw it on the fire, just to burn off the rest of the feathers. When the fire has burned down to ashes and coals, they bury the emu in the coals till he's cooked right through.'

Deaggidditt describes how emus are cooked in the ground oven Aboriginal people use for large game. Very few parts of the animal are wasted. The emu feathers are valuable being used both to decorate people's bodies for ceremonies and to make special shoes which don't leave tracks. These shoes are worn by 'clever men' on secret missions.
The spleen of the animal is, however, thrown away — it is the 'poison bag' Deaggidditt talks about.

Note: Before commencing the garment it is essential to check your tension (see below).

		S	M	L
To Fit	CM	76-81	86-91	97-102
Bust/Chest	INS	30-32	34-36	38-40
Actual	CM	106	116	127
Measurement	INS	42	46	50
Length to Back	CM	64	65	66
Neck (approx)	INS	25	25½	26
Sleeve Seam				
Women (approx)	CM	43	43	43
	INS	17	17	17
Men (approx)	CM	48	48	48
	INS	19	19	19

Note: This is a loose-fitting garment.

Materials

Cleckheaton Natural 8 Ply 50 g (2 oz) balls or equivalent yarn to give stated tension.

	S	M	L
MC (Black)	5	6	6
C1 (Grey)	6	6	7
C2 (White)	3	4	4
C3 (Khaki)	1	1	1
C4 (Blue)	1	2	2
C5 (Red)	1	1	1

Note: You may require an extra ball of MC for men's sizes.

1 pair each 4 mm (No. 8) and 3.25 mm (No. 10) knitting needles, or **the required size to give correct tension**;
1 stitch holder; bobbins; 7 buttons.

Tension

This garment has been designed at a tension of 22 sts to 10 cm (4 ins) over st st, using 4 mm (No. 8) needles.

Back

Using 3.25 mm (No. 10) needles and MC, cast on 55 (60, 66) sts, using C1, cast on 54 (59, 65) sts. 109 (119, 131) sts.
1st Row: Using appropriate colours: K2, *P1, K1, rep from * to last st, K1.
2nd Row: Using appropriate colours: K1, *P1, K1, rep from * to end.
Rep 1st and 2nd rows until band measures 8 cm (3 ins) from beg, ending with a 2nd row and inc (5 sts evenly in C1 section and 5 sts evenly in MC section) across last row. 119 (129, 141) sts. Change to 4 mm (No. 8) needles and beg patt. Work rows 1 to 160 (162, 166) inclusive from Graph A.

Shape shoulders

Keeping Graph correct, cast off 11 (12, 13) sts at beg of next 4 (4, 6) rows, then 10 (11, 12) sts at beg of foll 4 (4, 2) rows. Leave rem 35 (37, 39) sts on a stitch holder.

Left front

Using 3.25 mm (No. 10) needles and C1, cast on 55 (61, 67) sts. Work in rib as for lower band of Back, until band measures 8 cm (3 ins) from beg, ending with a 2nd row, and inc 4 (3, 3) sts evenly across last row. 59 (64, 70) sts.
Change to 4 mm (No. 8) needles and beg patt. Work rows 1 to 143 (143, 145) inclusive from Graph A as indicated for Left Front.

Shape neck

Keeping Graph correct, cast off 11 (11, 12) sts at beg of next row. Dec 1 st at neck edge in next and foll alt rows 6 (7, 7) times in all. Work 5 (5, 7) rows.

Shape shoulder

Cast off 11 (12, 13) sts at beg of next row and foll alt row, then 10 (11, 13) sts at beg of foll alt row. Work 1 row. Cast off.

Right front

To correspond with Left Front, using MC in place of C1 for lower band, and following Graph A for Right Front.

Left sleeve

Using 3.25 mm (No. 10) needles and C1, cast on 45 (47, 49) sts. Work in rib as for lower band of Back, until band measures 6 cm (2½ ins) from beg for **Women** or 7 cm (2¾ ins) from beg for **Men**, ending with a 2nd row and inc 12 sts evenly across last row. 57 (59, 61) sts.

Change to 4 mm (No. 8) needles and beg patt.
Work rows 1 to 104 inclusive from Graph B for **Women**, or rows 1 to 116 inclusive for **Men**, **at same time** inc 1 st at each end of 5th and foll 4th rows until there are 95 (103, 111) sts, **1st and 2nd Sizes Only** — then in foll 6th rows until there are 103 (107) sts.

Shape top

Keeping Graph correct, cast off 10 sts at beg of next 8 rows. Cast off rem sts.

Right sleeve

Work as for Left Sleeve, using Graph C instead of Graph B.

Buttonhole bands

Right front band for women, left front band for men

Using 3.25 mm (No. 10) needles and C1, cast on 9 sts. Work 4 rows rib as for lower band of Back.

Emu - Bush Food

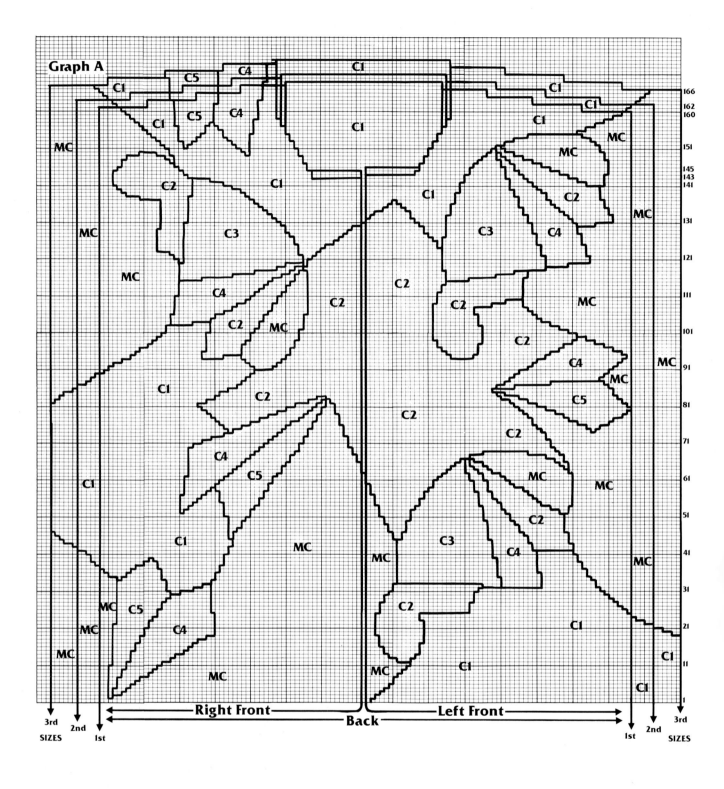

Graph A

MC · C1 · C5 · C4 · C1 · C1 · C1
166 · 162 · 160 · 151 · 145 · 143 · 141 · 131 · 121 · 111 · 101 · 91 · 81 · 71 · 61 · 51 · 41 · 31 · 21 · 11 · 1

3rd SIZES · 2nd · 1st — Right Front — Back — Left Front — 1st · 2nd · 3rd SIZES

5th Row: Rib 4, yfwd, K2tog, rib 3. Work 23 rows rib. Rep last 24 rows 5 times, then first 20 of these 24 rows once. 6 buttonholes. Leave sts on a spare needle.

Left front band for women, right front band for men

Work as for other Front Band omitting buttonholes.

Neckband

Using back-stitch, join shoulder seams. With right side facing, using 3.25 mm (No. 10) needles and C1, rib across Right Front Band sts, knit up 89 (95, 103) sts evenly around neck edge, including sts from stitch holder, then rib across Left Front Band sts. 107 (113, 121) sts. Work 3 rows rib.

Women: 4th Row Rib 4, yfwd, K2tog, rib to end.

Men: 4th Row Rib to last 5 sts, yfwd, K2tog, rib 3.

All sizes, Rib 3 rows. Cast off **loosely** in rib.

To make up

Using back-stitch, sew in Sleeves placing centre top of Sleeve to shoulder seam. Join side and Sleeve seams. Sew Front Bands in position stretching slightly to fit. Sew on buttons. Outline emu shapes in stem stitch in MC if desired.

Emu - Bush Food

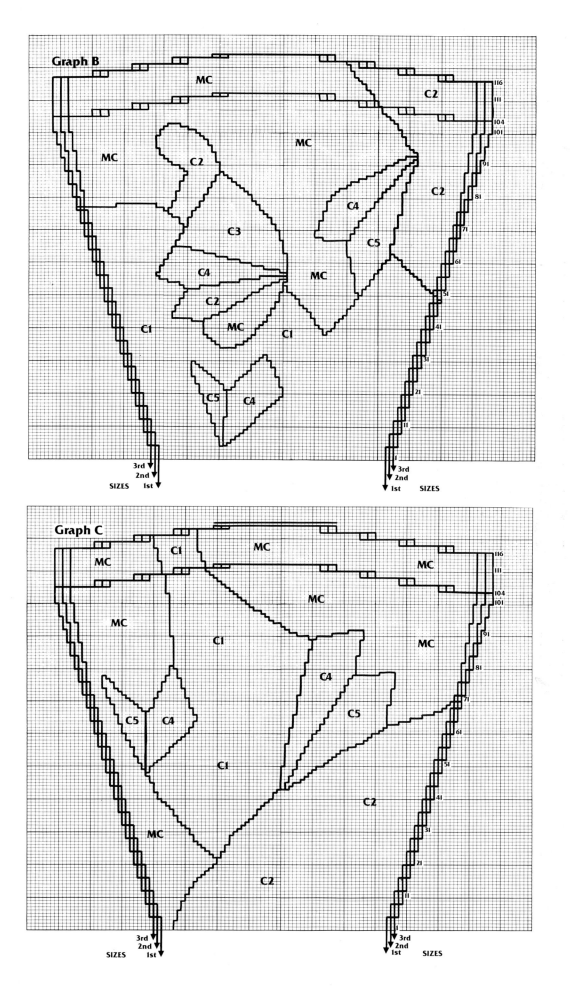

Papatjara - Dingoes

Papatjara - Dingoes

'Dingoes are the wild dogs of central Australia, but the people have always had them to help in the hunting. My grandfather was chased up a tree by a mob of wild dingoes. He was out hunting. He had to call out for help, and they had to set fire to the spinifex grass to frighten off the dingoes.'

Deaggidditt had told an everyday story about the dingo, but this dog is also an important part of Aboriginal mythology having been on the Australian continent as long as Aboriginal people. In this simple design, Deaggidditt uses the X-ray style of Aboriginal painting by showing another colour through the dingoes' bodies. The green areas indicate campsites, waterholes and more fertile country on the nomadic trail.

Note: Before commencing the garment it is essential to check your tension (see below).

To Fit		S	M	L
To Fit	CM	76-81	86-91	97-102
Bust/Chest	INS	30-32	34-36	38-40
Actual	CM	106	116	127
Measurement	INS	42	46	50
Length to	CM	64	65	66
Back Neck	INS	25	25½	26
Sleeve Seam				
Women (approx)	CM	43	43	43
	INS	17	17	17
Men (approx)	CM	48	48	48
	INS	19	19	19

Note: This is a loose-fitting garment.

Materials

Cleckheaton 8 Ply Machine Wash 50 g (2 oz) balls **or equivalent yarn to give stated tension.**

	S	M	L
MC (Blue)	9	10	11
C1 (Pink)	2	2	2
C2 (Green)	2	2	2
C3 (Yellow)	1	1	1

Note: You may require an extra ball of MC for men's sizes.

1 pair each 4 mm (No. 8) 3.25 mm (No. 10) and 1 set of 3.25 mm (No. 10) knitting needles, or **the required size to give correct tension;** 2 stitch holders; bobbins.

Tension

This garment has been designed at a tension of 22 sts to 10 cm (4 ins) over st st, using 4 mm (No. 8) needles.

Back

Using 3.25 mm (No. 10) needles and MC, cast on 105 (115, 127) sts.
1st Row: K2, *P1, K1, rep from * to last st, K1.
2nd Row: K1, *P1, K1, rep from * to end.
Rep 1st and 2nd rows until band measures 6 cm (2½ ins) from beg, ending with a 2nd row and inc 13 sts evenly across last row. 118 (128, 140) sts.
Change to 4 mm (No. 8) needles.** Work rows 1 to 174 (176, 178) inclusive from Graph A.

Shape shoulders

Keeping Graph A correct, cast off 10 (11, 13) sts at beg of next 6 rows, then 11 (12, 11) sts at beg of foll 2 rows. Leave rem 36 (38, 40) sts on a stitch holder.

Front

Work as for Back to **. Work rows 1 to 156 inclusive from Graph A.

Shape neck

Keeping Graph A correct,
Next Row: K47 (52, 58), **turn.**
Dec 1 st at left neck edge in alt rows 6 (7, 8) times. 41 (45, 50) sts rem. Work 5 rows.

Shape shoulder

Keeping Graph A correct, cast off 10 (11, 13) sts at beg of next and foll alt rows 3 times in all. Work 1 row. Cast off. Slip next 24 sts onto a stitch holder and leave. Join yarn to rem sts at right neck edge and complete to correspond with left side.

Sleeves

Using 3.25 mm (No. 10) needles and MC, cast on 45 (47, 49) sts. Work in rib as for lower band of Back until band measures 6 cm (2½ ins) from beg, ending with a 2nd

row and inc 15 sts evenly across last row. 60 (62, 64) sts.
Change to 4 mm (No. 8) needles. Cont in st st (1 row K, 1 row P), inc 1 st at each end of 3rd and foll 4th row. 64 (66, 68) sts. Work 3 rows. Work rows 1 to 74 inclusive from Graph B, at the same time, inc 1 st at each end of next and foll 4th rows until there are 86 (94, 102) sts, then in foll 6th rows until there are 96 (100, 104) sts. Using MC, cont in st st, inc 1 st at each end of 3rd and foll 6th rows until there are 102 (106, 110) sts. Cont without shaping until side edge measures 43 cm (17 ins) for **Women** or 48 cm (19 ins) for **Men**, ending with a purl row.

Shape top

Cast off 10 sts at beg of next 8 rows. Cast off rem sts.

Neckband

Using back-stitch, join shoulder seams.

Graph B

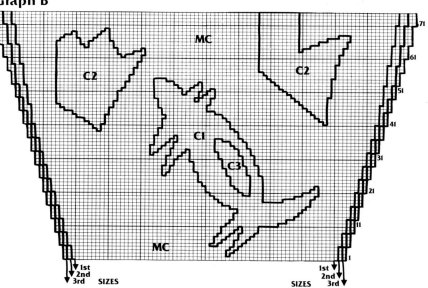

Papatjara - Dingoes

Graph A

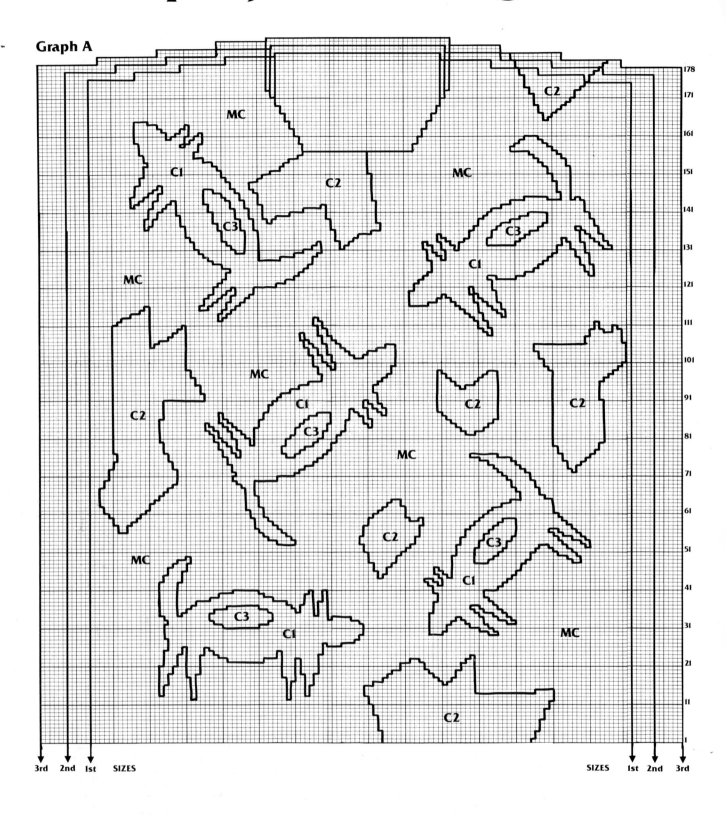

With right side facing, using set of
3.25 mm (No. 10) needles and MC, beg at
left shoulder seam, knit up 96 (102, 108)
sts, evenly around neck edge, including sts
from stitch holders.
1st Round: *K1, P1, rep from * to end.
Rep 1st round until neckband measures
5 cm (2 ins) from beg. Cast off **loosely**
in rib.

To make up

Using back-stitch, sew in Sleeves placing
centre top of Sleeve to shoulder seam. Join
side and Sleeve seams. Fold Neckband in
half onto wrong side and slip-stitch in
position.

Mamu - Spirit

Mamu - Spirit

'*One time my grandfather went hunting in winter time. He seen a cloud forming up, like rain, so he made a camp and when he had just finished putting up a shelter, it started raining. He lit a small fire and sat down next to it. Then he could hear loud footsteps and splashes, he could hear this* mamu *spirit coming up. My grandfather had left his spear by the door. The* mamu *came right up, and lay down by the fire. My grandfather started getting cold. He was so scared he couldn't move, or sing out. In the morning the* mamu *took off.*'

This story is about a malevolent spirit who can only be glimpsed in passing by humans. Such spirits are all over Aboriginal Australia, in different forms and with different names, but this one is from the Western Desert. The *mamu* is partially human in form, as the design shows.

Note: Before commencing the garment it is essential to check your tension (see below).

		S	M	L
To Fit	CM	76-81	86-91	97-102
Bust/Chest	INS	30-32	34-36	38-40
Actual	CM	106	116	127
Measurement	INS	42	46	50
Length to Back	CM	64	65	66
Neck (approx)	INS	25	25½	26
Sleeve Seam				
Women (approx)	CM	43	43	43
	INS	17	17	17
Men (approx)	CM	48	48	48
	INS	19	19	19

Note: This is a loose-fitting garment.

Materials

Cleckheaton 8 Ply Machine Wash 50 g (2 oz) balls **or equivalent yarn to give stated tension.**

	S	M	L
MC (Black)	10	11	12
C1 (White)	1	1	1

Note: You may require an extra ball of MC for men's sizes.
1 pair each 3.75 mm (No. 9) and 3 mm (No. 11) and 1 set of 3 mm (No. 11) knitting needles, **or the required size to give correct tension**; 2 stitch holders; bobbins.

Tension

This garment has been designed at a tension of 26 sts to 10 cm (4 ins) over st st, using 3.75 mm (No. 9) needles.

Front

Using 3 mm (No. 11) needles and MC, cast on 125 (137, 153) sts.
1st Row: K2, *P1, K1, rep from * to last st, K1.
2nd row: K1, *P1, K1, rep from * to end.
Rep 1st and 2nd rows until band measures 6 cm (2½ ins) from beg, ending with a 2nd row and inc 14 sts evenly across last row. 139 (151, 167) sts.
Change to 3.75 mm (No. 9) needles.**
Work rows 1 to 178 inclusive from Graph. Using MC, work 2 rows st st (1 row K, 1 row P).

Shape neck

Next Row: K57 (62, 70), **turn.**
Dec 1 st at left neck edge in alt rows 8 (9, 10) times. 49 (53, 60) sts rem. Work 3 rows.

Shape shoulder

Cast off 12 (13, 15) sts at beg of next and foll alt rows 3 times in all. Work 1 row. Cast off. Slip next 25 (27, 27) sts onto a stitch holder and leave. Join yarn to rem sts at right neck edge and complete to correspond with left side.

Back

Work as for Front to **. Using MC only, work in st st until Back measures same as Front to shoulder shaping.

Shape shoulders

Cast off 12 (13, 15) sts at beg of next 6 rows, then 13 (14, 15) sts at beg of foll 2 rows. Leave rem 41 (45, 47) sts on a stitch holder.

Sleeves

Using 3 mm (No. 11) needles and MC, cast on 53 (55, 57) sts. Work in rib as for lower band of Back until band measures 6 cm (2½ ins) from beg, ending with a 2nd row and inc 16 sts evenly across last row. 69 (71, 73) sts.
Change to 3.75 mm (No. 9) needles. Cont in st st, inc 1 st at each end of 3rd and foll 4th (4th, alt) rows until there are 107 (121, 79) sts, then in foll 6th (6th, 4th) rows until there are 119 (125, 131) sts. Cont without shaping until side edge measures 43 cm (17 ins) for **Women**, or 48 cm (19 ins) for **Men**, ending with a purl row.

Shape top

Cast off 13 sts at beg of next 8 rows. Cast off rem sts.

Neckband

Using back-stitch, join shoulder seams. With right side facing, using set of 3 mm

(No. 11) needles and MC, beg at left shoulder seam, knit up 106 (116, 122) sts evenly around neck edge (including sts from stitch holders).
1st Round: *K1, P1, rep from * to end. Rep 1st round until Neckband measures 5 cm (2 ins) from beg. Cast off **loosely** in rib.

To make up

Using back-stitch, sew in Sleeves placing centre top of Sleeve to shoulder seam. Join side and Sleeve seams. Fold Neckband in half onto wrong side and slip-stitch in position.

Mamu - Spirit

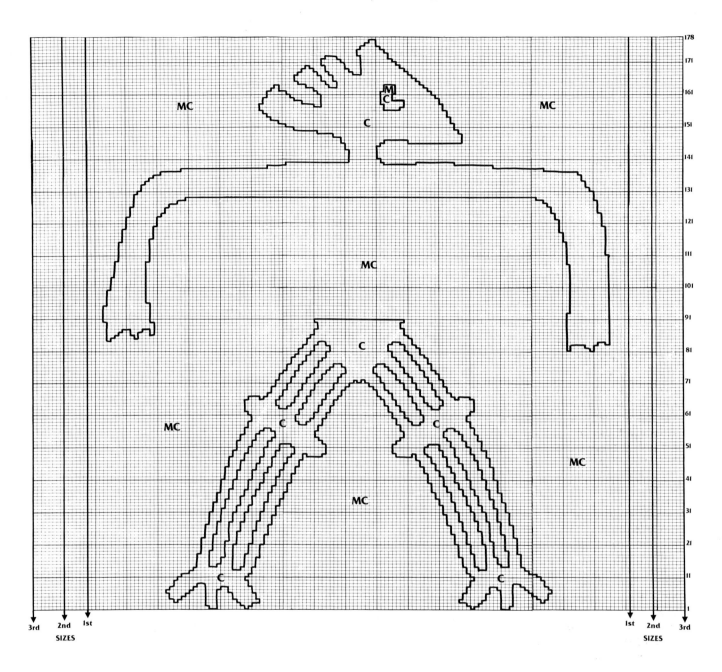

Kukaku - Hunting Time

Kukaku - Hunting Time

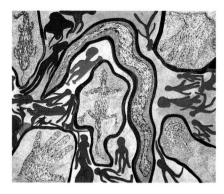

'When I was a little kid we would always hunt little lizards and cook them on our camp fire, just like the adults. This is how we learnt to hunt.'

Goannas and various other sorts of lizards are a constant source of food for Aboriginal peoples throughout the continent. Cooked over the hot coals of the campfire, goannas produce a delicious poultry-like flesh. In this design Deaggidditt has used different areas of colour to separate the hunter from the hunted goanna.

Note: Before commencing the garment it is essential to check your tension (see below).

		S	M	L
To Fit	CM	76-81	86-91	97-102
Bust/Chest	INS	30-32	34-36	38-40
Actual	CM	106	116	127
Measurement	INS	42	46	50
Length to Back	CM	64	65	66
Neck (approx)	INS	25	25½	26
Sleeve Seam				
Women (approx)	CM	43	43	43
	INS	17	17	17
Men (approx)	CM	48	48	48
	INS	19	19	19

Note: This is a loose-fitting garment.

Materials

Cleckheaton Natural 8 Ply 50 g (2 oz) balls or equivalent yarn to give stated tension.

	S	M	L
MC (Green)	6	6	7
C1 (White)	4	5	5
C2 (Sand)	3	3	3
C3 (Rust)	1	1	1
C4 (Brown)	1	1	1
C5 (Taupe)	1	1	1

Note: You may require an extra ball of MC for men's sizes.

1 pair each 4 mm (No. 8) and 3.25 mm (No. 10), and 1 set of 3.25 mm (No. 10), and 1 set of 3.25 mm (No. 10) knitting needles, or **the required size to give correct tension**; 2 stitch holders; bobbins.

Tension

This garment has been designed at a tension of 22 sts to 10 cm (4 ins) over st st, using 4 mm (No. 8) needles.

Note: When working from Graph for Back, read odd numbered rows (knit rows) from left to right, and even numbered rows (purl rows) from right to left.
When working from Graph for Front and Sleeves, read odd numbered rows (knit rows) from right to left, and even numbered rows (purl rows) from left to right.

Back

Using 3.25 mm (No. 10) needles and MC, cast on 103 (113, 125) sts.
1st Row: K2, *P1, K1, rep from * to last st, K1.
2nd Row: K1, *P1, K1, rep from * to end.
Rep 1st and 2nd rows until band measures 8 cm (3 ins) from beg, ending with a 2nd row and inc 16 sts evenly across last row. 119 (129, 141) sts.
Change to 4 mm (No. 8) needles and beg patt. ** Work rows 1 to 148 (152, 154) inclusive from Graph A.

Shape shoulders

Cast off 11 (12, 13) sts at beg of next 4 (4, 6) rows, then 10 (11, 12) sts at beg of foll 4 (4, 2) rows. Leave rem 35 (37, 39) sts on a stitch holder.

Front

Work as for Back to **. Work rows 1 to 130 (132, 134) inclusive from Graph A.

Shape neck

Keeping Graph correct,
Next Row: K48 (53, 58), **turn**.
Dec 1 st at neck edge in alt rows 6 (7, 7) times. 42 (46, 51) sts rem. Work 5 rows.

Shape shoulder

Cast off 11 (12, 13) sts at beg of next row and foll alt row, then 10 (11, 13) sts at beg of foll alt row. Work 1 row. Cast off. Slip next 23 (23, 25) sts onto a stitch holder and leave. Join yarn to rem sts and complete right hand side of neck to correspond with left side.

Right sleeve

Using 3.25 mm (No. 10) needles and C1, cast on 43 (45, 47) sts. Work in rib as for lower band of Back, until band measures 8 cm (3 ins) from beg, ending with a 2nd row and inc 14 sts evenly across last row. 57 (59, 61) sts.
Change to 4 mm (No. 8) needles and beg patt. Work rows 1 to 98 inclusive from Graph B for **Women**, or rows 1 to 112 inclusive for **Men, at same time** inc 1 st at each end of 5th and foll 4th (alt, alt) rows until there are 101 (63, 69) sts, then in foll 6th (4th, 4th) row/s until there are 103 (107, 111) sts.

Shape top

Keeping Graph correct, cast off 10 sts at beg of next 8 rows. Cast off rem sts.

Left sleeve

Work as for Right Sleeve, using MC only and working in st st (1 row K, 1 row P) throughout.

Neckband

Using back-stitch, join shoulder seams. With right side facing, using set of 3.25 mm (No. 10) needles and C1, knit up 96 (102, 110) sts evenly around neck edge, including sts from stitch holders.
1st Round: *K1, P1, rep from * to end.
Rep 1st round 9 times. Cast off **loosely** in rib.

To make up

Using back-stitch, sew in Sleeves placing centre top of Sleeve to shoulder seam. Join side and Sleeve seams.

Kukaku - Hunting Time

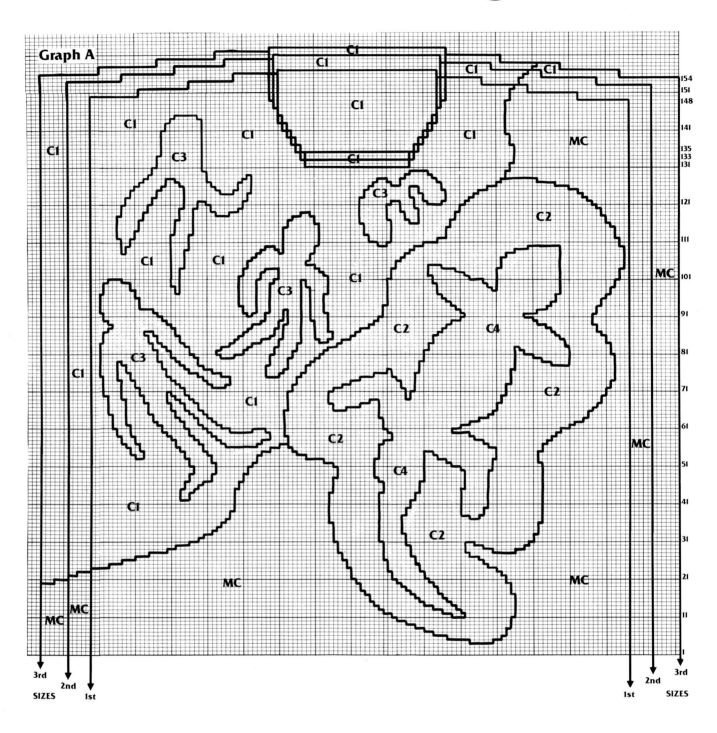

Kukaku - Hunting Time

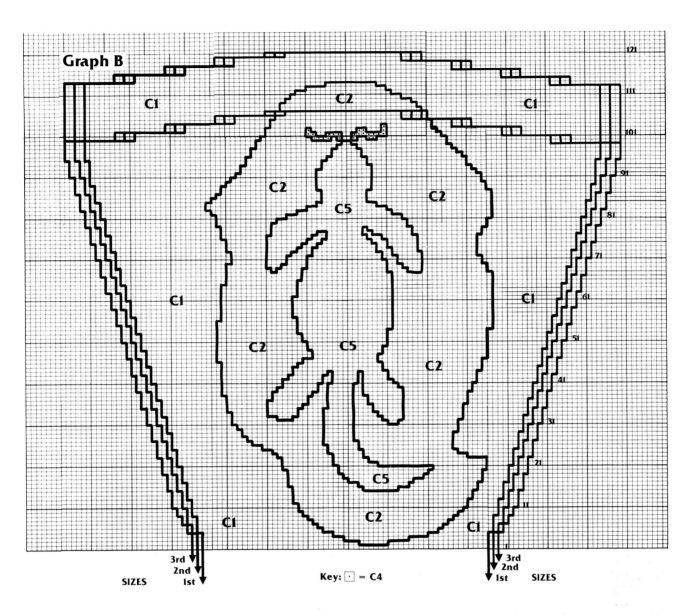

Mother and Baby

Mother and Baby

'*I first made this drawing with texta on paper. It's a memory of things I have seen in daily life around the camp where my people live.*'

This dramatic design tells us of the importance of human relationships for Aborigines. Deaggidditt has represented the mother/child relationship as if it were on a cave wall, or a drawing in the sand.

Note: Before commencing the garment it is essential to check your tension (see below).

		S	M	L
To Fit	CM	76–81	86–91	97–102
Bust/Chest	INS	30–32	34–36	38–40
Actual	CM	106	116	127
Measurement	INS	42	46	50
Length to Back	CM	64	65	66
Neck (approx)	INS	25	25½	26
Sleeve Seam				
Women (approx)	CM	43	43	43
	INS	17	17	17
Men (approx)	CM	48	48	48
	INS	19	19	19

Note: This is a loose-fitting garment.

Materials

Cleckheaton 8 Ply Machine Wash 50 g (2 oz) balls **or equivalent yarn to give stated tension.**

	S	M	L
MC (Black)	12	13	14
C1 (White)	1	1	1

Note: You may require an extra ball of MC for men's sizes.
1 pair each 4 mm (No. 8) and 3.25 mm (No. 10), and 1 set of 3.25 mm (No. 10) knitting needles, or **the required size to give correct tension**; 2 stitch holders; bobbins.

Tension

This garment has been designed at a tension of 22 sts to 10 cm (4 ins) over st st, using 4 mm (No. 8) needles.

Front

Using 3.25 mm (No. 10) needles and MC, cast on 105 (115, 127) sts.
1st Row: K2, *P1, K1 rep from * to last st, K1.
2nd Row: K1, *P1, K1, rep from * to end.
Rep 1st and 2nd rows until band measures 6 cm (2½ ins) from beg, ending with a 2nd row and inc 13 sts evenly across last row. 118 (128, 140) sts.
Change to 4 mm (No. 8) needles. ** Work rows 1 to 154 inclusive from Graph. Using MC, work 2 rows st st (1 row K, 1 row P).

Shape neck

Next Row: K47 (52, 58) **turn.**
Dec 1 st at left neck edge in alt rows 6 (7, 8) times. 41 (45, 50) sts rem. Work 5 rows.

Shape shoulder

Cast off 10 (11, 13) sts at beg of next and foll alt rows 3 times in all. Work 1 row. Cast off. Slip next 24 sts onto a stitch holder and leave. Join yarn to rem sts at right neck edge and complete to correspond with left side.

Back

Work as for Front to **. Work 174 (176, 178) rows st st.

Shape shoulders

Cast off 10 (11, 13) sts at beg of next 6 rows, then 11 (12, 11) sts at beg of foll 2 rows. Leave rem 36 (38, 40) sts on a stitch holder.

Sleeves

Using 3.25 mm (No. 10) needles and MC, cast on 45 (47, 49) sts.
Work in rib as for lower band of Front until band measures 6 cm (2½ ins) from beg, ending with a 2nd row and inc 15 sts evenly across last row. 60 (62, 64) sts.
Change to 4 mm (No. 8) needles. Cont in st st, inc 1 st at each end of 3rd row and foll 4th rows until there are 86 (94, 102) sts, then in foll 6th rows until there are 102 (106, 110) sts. Cont without shaping until side edge measures 43 cm (17 ins) for **Women** or 48 cm (19 ins) for **Men**, ending with a purl row.

Shape top

Cast off 10 sts at beg of next 8 rows.
Cast off rem sts.

Neckband

Using back-stitch, join shoulder seams. With right side facing, using set of 3.25 mm (No. 10) needles and MC, beg at

left shoulder seam, knit up 96 (102, 108) sts evenly around neck edge (including sts from stitch holders).
1st Round: *K1, P1, rep from * to end.
Rep 1st round until Neckband measures 5 cm (2 ins) from beg. Cast off **loosely** in rib.

To make up

Using back-stitch, sew in Sleeves placing centre top of Sleeve to shoulder seam. Join side and Sleeve seams. Fold Neckband in half onto wrong side and slip-stitch in position.

Mother and Baby

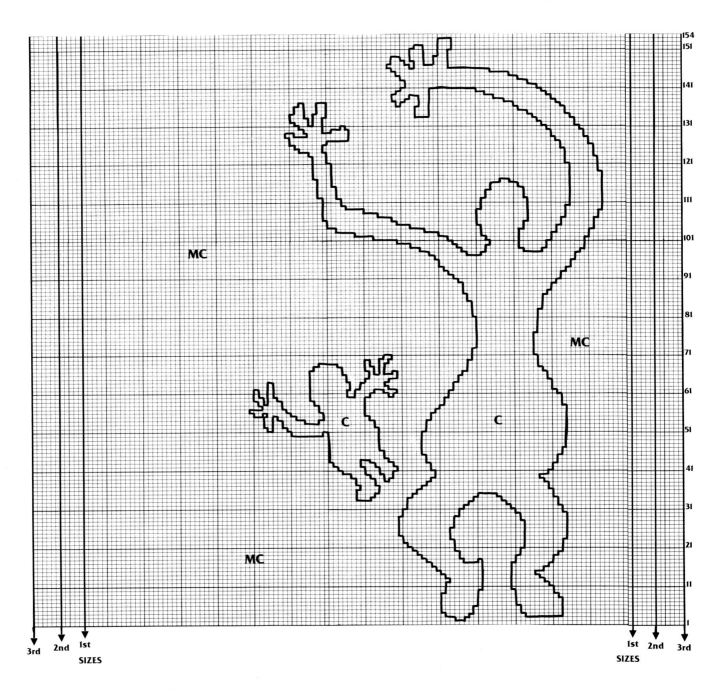

Kalya - Emu Chicks

Kalya - Emu Chicks

This large ostrich-like bird cannot fly, but can out-distance any other Australian native animal. The male and female birds live monogamously, and while the female can lay up to a dozen eggs — each of which has the contents of a dozen hen's eggs — the male looks after the nest. These large grey birds can be seen on the open plains searching for vegetable foods and grubs, while the little chicks, quite differently coloured with brown and grey stripes, follow along behind.

Note: Before commencing the garment it is essential to check your tension (see below).

		S	M	L
To Fit	CM	76-81	86-91	97-102
Bust/Chest	INS	30-32	34-36	38-40
Actual	CM	106	116	127
Measurement	INS	42	46	50
Length to Back	CM	68	69	70
Neck (approx)	INS	27	27	27½
Sleeve Seam				
Women (approx)	CM	43	43	43
	INS	17	17	17
Men (approx)	CM	48	48	48
	INS	19	19	19

Note: This is a loose-fitting garment.

Materials

Cleckheaton Natural 8 Ply 50 g (2 oz) balls or equivalent yarns to give stated tension.

	S	M	L
MC (Rust)	12	13	14
C1 (Dark Brown)	1	1	1
C3 (Sand)	1	1	1
C4 (Khaki)	1	1	1

AND **Cleckheaton 8 Ply Machine Wash** 50 g (2 oz) balls or equivalent yarn to give stated tension.

C2 (Coral)	1	1	1

You may require an extra ball of MC for men's sizes.

1 pair each 4 mm (No. 8), 3.25 mm (No. 10) and 1 set of 3.25 mm (No. 10) knitting needles, or **the required size to give correct tension;** 2 stitch holders; bobbins.

Note: Natural 8 Ply is not machine washable.

Tension

This garment has been designed at a tension of 22 sts to 10 cm (4 ins) over st st, using 4 mm (No. 8) needles.

Back

Using 3.25 mm (No. 10) needles and MC, cast on 105 (115, 127) sts.
1st Row: K2, *P1, K1, rep from * to last st, K1.
2nd Row: K1, *P1, K1, rep from * to end.
Rep 1st and 2nd rows until band measures 6 cm (2½ ins) from beg, ending with a 2nd row and inc 13 sts, evenly across last row. 118 (128, 140) sts.
Change to 4 mm (No. 8) needles.** Work rows 1 to 174 (176, 178) inclusive from Graph A.

Shape shoulders

Cast off 10 (11, 13) sts at beg of next 6 rows, then 11 (12, 11) sts at beg of foll 2 rows. Leave rem 36 (38, 40) sts on a stitch holder.

Front

Work as for Back to **. Work rows 1 to 156 inclusive from Graph A.

Shape neck

Keeping Graph A correct,
Next Row: K47 (52, 58), **turn.**
Dec 1 st at left neck edge in alt rows 6 (7, 8) times. 41 (45, 50) sts rem. Work 5 rows.

Shape shoulder

Cast off 10 (11, 13) sts at beg of next and foll alt rows 3 times in all. Work 1 row. Cast off. Slip next 24 sts onto a stitch holder and leave. Join yarn to rem sts at right neck edge and complete to correspond with left side of neck.

Sleeves

Using 3.25 mm (No. 10) needles and MC, cast on 45 (47, 49) sts. Work in rib as for lower band of Back until band measures 6 cm (2½ ins) from beg, ending with a 2nd row and inc 15 sts evenly across last row. 60 (62, 64) sts.
Change to 4 mm (No. 8) needles. Cont in st st (1 row K, 1 row P) inc 1 st at each end

Graph B

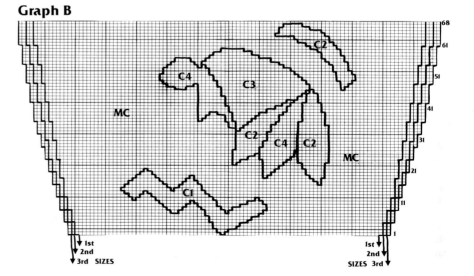

Kalya - Emu Chicks

Graph A

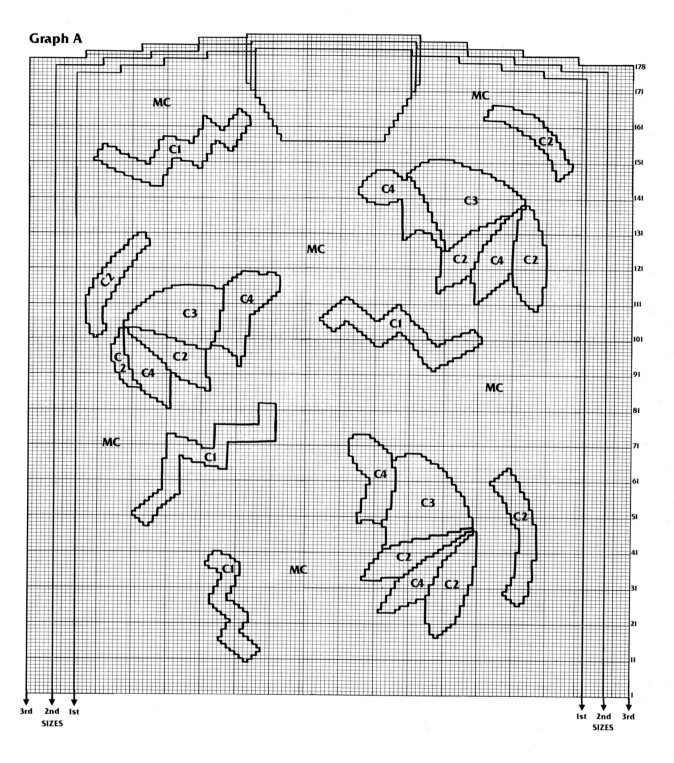

of 3rd row and foll 4th rows until there are 78 (80, 82) sts.

Work 3 rows. Work rows 1 to 68 inclusive from Graph B, **at same time**, inc 1 st at each end of next row and foll 4th rows until there are 86 (94, 102) sts, then in foll 6th rows until there are 102 (106, 110) sts. Using MC, cont in st st until side edge measures 43 cm (17 ins) for **Women**, and 48 cm (19 ins) for **Men**, ending with a purl row.

Shape top

Cast of 10 sts at beg of next 8 rows. Cast off rem sts.

Neckband

Using back-stitch, join shoulder seams. With right side facing, using set of 3.25 mm (No. 10) needles and MC, beg at left shoulder seam, knit up 96 (102, 108) sts evenly around neck edge, including sts from stitch holders.

1st Round: *K1, P1, rep from * to end. Rep 1st round until Neckband measures 5 cm (2 ins) from beg. Cast off **loosely** in rib.

To make up

Using back-stitch, sew in Sleeves placing centre top of Sleeve to shoulder seam. Join side and Sleeve seams. Fold Neckband in half onto wrong side and slip-stitch in position.

Seven Emu Sisters

Seven Emu Sisters

One Aboriginal legend, about the Seven Emu Sisters, tells how the sisters were pursued by dingo men. These men started a bushfire to flush them from their hiding place. The long wings which the emus had at that time were burnt so badly they could no longer fly, and their strenuous efforts to escape the burning grass made their legs long and swift.

Note: Before commencing the garment it is essential to check your tension (see below).

		S	M	L
To Fit	CM	76-81	86-91	97-102
Bust/Chest	INS	30-32	34-36	38-40
Actual	CM	106	116	127
Measurement	INS	42	46	50
Length to Back	CM	64	65	66
Neck (approx)	INS	25	25½	26
Sleeve Seam				
Women (approx)	CM	43	43	43
	INS	17	17	17
Men (approx)	CM	48	48	48
	INS	19	19	19

Note: This is a loose-fitting garment.

Materials

Cleckheaton 8 Ply Machine Wash 50 g (2 oz) balls or equivalent yarn to give stated tension.

	S	M	L
MC (Pink)	8	9	10
C1 (Purple)	3	3	3
C2 (Red	1	1	1
C3 (Yellow)	1	1	1
C4 (Jade)	1	1	1
C5 (Blue)	1	1	1
C6 (Black)	1	1	1

Note: You may require an extra ball of MC for men's sizes.
1 pair each 4 mm (No. 8) and 3.25 mm (No. 10) knitting needles, or **the required size to give correct tension**; 1 stitch holder; bobbins; 8 buttons.

Tension

This garment has been designed at a tension of 22 sts to 10 cm (4 ins) over st st, using 4 mm (No. 8) needles.

Back

Using 3.25 mm (No. 10) needles and MC, cast on 109 (119, 131) sts.
1st Row: K2, *P1, K1, rep from * to last st, K1.

2nd Row: K1, *P1, K1, rep from * to end.
Rep 1st and 2nd rows until band measures 8 cm (3 ins) from beg, ending with a 2nd row and inc 10 sts evenly across last row. 119 (129, 141) sts.
Change to 4 mm (No. 8) needles and beg patt. Work rows 1 to 160 (162, 166) inclusive from Graph A.

Shape shoulders

Keeping graph correct, cast off 11 (12, 13) sts at beg of next 4 (4, 6) rows, then 10 (11, 12) sts at beg of foll 4 (4, 2) rows. Leave rem 35 (37, 39) sts on a stitch holder.

Left front

Using 3.25 mm (No. 10) needles and MC, cast on 55 (61, 67) sts. Work in rib as for lower band of Back until band measures 8 cm (3 ins) from beg, ending with a 2nd row, and inc 4 (3, 3) sts evenly across last row. 59 (64, 70) sts. Change to 4 mm (No. 8) needles and beg patt. Work rows 1 to 143 (143, 145) inclusive from Graph A for Left Front.

Shape neck

Keeping Graph correct, cast off 11 (11, 12) sts at beg of next row. Dec 1 st at neck edge in next and foll alt rows 6 (7, 7) times in all. 42 (46, 51) sts. Work 5 (5, 7) rows.

Shape shoulder

Cast off 11 (12, 13) sts at beg of next row and foll alt row, then 10 (11, 13) sts at beg of foll alt row. Work 1 row. Cast off.

Right front

To correspond with Left Front, following Graph A for Right Front.

Graph B

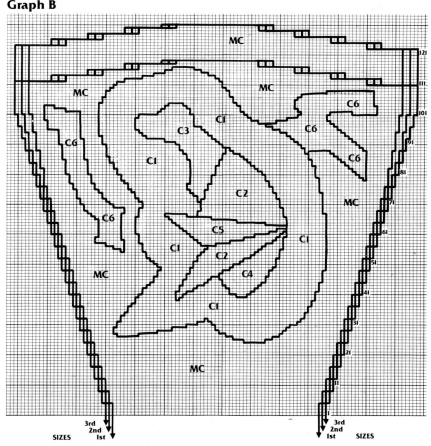

Seven Emu Sisters

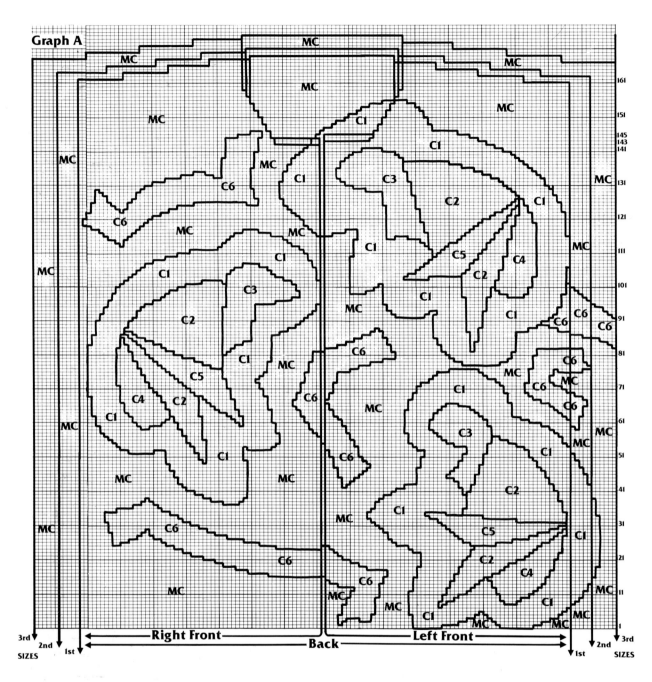

Graph A

Right Front — Back — Left Front

3rd SIZES   2nd   1st   1st   2nd   3rd SIZES

Sleeves

Using 3.25 mm (No. 10) needles and MC, cast on 45 (47, 49) sts. Work in rib as for lower band of Back until band measures 6 cm (2½ ins) from beg for **Women** or 7 cm (2¾ ins) from beg for **Men**, ending with a 2nd row and inc 12 sts evenly across last row. 57 (59, 61) sts. Change to 4 mm (No. 8) needles and beg patt. Work rows 1 to 110 inclusive from Graph B for **Women**, or rows 1 to 122 inclusive for **Men, at same time** inc 1 st at each end of 5th and foll 4th rows until there are 95 (103, 111) sts, **1st and 2nd Sizes Only** — cont inc in foll 6th rows until there are 103 (107) sts.

Shape top

Keeping Graph correct, cast off 10 sts at beg of next 8 rows. Cast off rem sts.

Buttonhole bands

Right front band for women, left front band for men

Using 3.25 mm (No. 10) needles and MC, cast on 11 sts. Work 4 rows rib as for lower band of Back.
5th Row: Rib 5, yfwd, K2tog, rib 4.
Work 27 rows rib. Rep last 28 rows 5 times more, then first 24 of these 28 rows once. 7 buttonholes. Leave sts on a spare needle.

Left front band for women, right front band for men

Work as for other Front Band omitting buttonholes.

Neckband

Using back-stitch, join shoulder seams.

With right side facing, using 3.25 mm (No. 10) needles and MC, rib across Right Front Band sts, knit up 89 (95, 103) sts evenly around neck edge, including sts from stitch holder then rib across Left Front Band sts. 111 (117, 125) sts. Work 3 rows rib.
Women: 4th Row Rib 4, fwd, K2tog, rib to end.
Men: 4th Row Rib to last 5 sts, yfwd, K2tog, rib 3.
All sizes, rib 5 rows. Cast off **loosely** in rib.

To make up

Using back-stitch, sew in Sleeves placing centre top of Sleeve to shoulder seam. Join side and Sleeve seams. Sew Front Bands in position stretching slightly to fit. Sew on buttons.

Maratjara - Many Hands

Maratjara - Many Hands

'To the north of my country, the people make these hand prints on rock walls. Sometimes you might see a hand with one or two fingers missing.'

If you visit the sites of cave paintings virtually anywhere in Aboriginal Australia you will often see 'stencils' made by people placing their hands on the cave wall and spraying white ochre from their mouths over their hands creating silhouettes. This ancient form of art is the inspiration for this design.

Note: Before commencing the garment it is essential to check your tension (see below).

		S	M	L
To Fit	CM	76–81	86–91	97–102
Bust/Chest	INS	30–32	34–36	38–40
Actual	CM	106	116	127
Measurement	INS	42	46	50
Length to Back	CM	64	65	66
Neck (approx)	INS	25	25½	26
Sleeve Seam				
Women (approx)	CM	43	43	43
	INS	17	17	17
Men (approx)	CM	48	48	48
	INS	19	19	19

Note: This is a loose-fitting garment.

Materials

Cleckheaton Natural 8 Ply 50 g (2 oz) balls or equivalent yarns to give stated tension.

	S	M	L
MC (Khaki)	5	6	6
C1 (Black)	3	3	4

AND **Cleckheaton The Boutique Collection Merino 8 Ply** 50 g (2 oz) balls

C2 (Cerise)	4	4	4

AND **Cleckheaton 8 Ply Machine Wash** 50 g (2 oz) balls

C3 (Mauve)	2	2	2

or equivalent yarns to give stated tension.

Note: You may require an extra ball of MC for men's sizes.
1 pair each 4 mm (No. 8) and 3.25 mm (No. 10), and 1 set of 3.25 mm (No. 10) knitting needles, or **the required size to give correct tension**; 2 stitch holders; bobbins.

Note: Natural 8 Ply and Merino 8 Ply are not machine washable.

Tension

This garment has been designed at a tension of 22 sts to 10 cm (4 ins) over st st, using 4 mm (No. 8) needles.

Abbreviations

'Bobble' = (K1, P1, K1, P1) all in next st, **turn**, P4, **turn**, K4, **turn**, P4, **turn**, K4, pass 2nd, 3rd and 4th sts over 1st.

Back

Using 3.25 mm (No. 10) needles and MC, cast on 103 (113, 125) sts.
1st Row: K2, *P1, K1, rep from * to last st, K1.
2nd Row: K1, *P1, K1, rep from * to end.
Rep 1st and 2nd rows until band measures 8 cm (3 ins) from beg, ending with a 2nd row and inc 16 sts evenly across last row. 119 (129, 141) sts.
Change to 4 mm (No. 8) needles and beg patt.** Work rows 1 to 148 (152, 154) inclusive from Graph A.

Shape shoulders

Cast off 11 (12, 13) sts at beg of next 4 (4, 6) rows, then 10 (11, 12) sts at beg of foll 4 (4, 2) rows. Leave rem 35 (37, 39) sts on a stitch holder

Front

Work as for Back to **. Work rows 1 to 130 (132, 132) inclusive from Graph A.

Shape neck

Keeping Graph correct,
Next Row: K48 (53, 58), **turn**.
Dec 1 st at left neck edge in alt rows 6 (7, 7) times. 42 (46, 51) sts. Work 5 (5, 7) rows.

Shape shoulder

Cast off 11 (12, 13) sts at beg of next row and foll alt row, then 10 (11, 13) sts at beg of foll alt row.
Work 1 row. Cast off. Slip next 23 (23, 25) sts onto a stitch holder and leave. Join yarn to rem sts and complete right hand side of neck to correspond with left side.

Right sleeve

Using 3.25 mm (No. 10) needles and MC, cast on 43 (45, 47) sts.
Work in rib as for lower band of Back until band measures 8 cm (3 ins) from beg, ending with a 2nd row and inc 14 sts evenly across last row. 57 (59, 61) sts.
Change to 4 mm (No. 8) needles. Work rows 1 to 98 inclusive from Graph B for **Women**, or rows 1 to 112 inclusive for **Men, at same time** inc 1 st at each end of 5th and foll 4th (alt, alt) rows until there are 101 (63, 69) sts, then in foll 6th (4th, 4th) row/s until there are 103 (107, 111) sts.

Shape top

Keeping Graph correct, cast off 10 sts at beg of next 8 rows. Cast off rem sts.

Left sleeve

Work as for Right Sleeve, using Graph C instead of Graph B.

Neckband

Using back-stitch, join shoulder seams. With right side facing, using set of 3.25 mm (No. 10) needles and MC, knit up 92 (98, 106) sts evenly around neck edge, including sts from stitch holders.
1st Round: *K1, P1, rep from * to end. Rep 1st round 9 times. Cast off **loosely** in rib.

To make up

Using back-stitch, sew in Sleeves placing centre top of Sleeve to shoulder seam. Join side and Sleeve seams.

Maratjara - Many Hands

Graph A

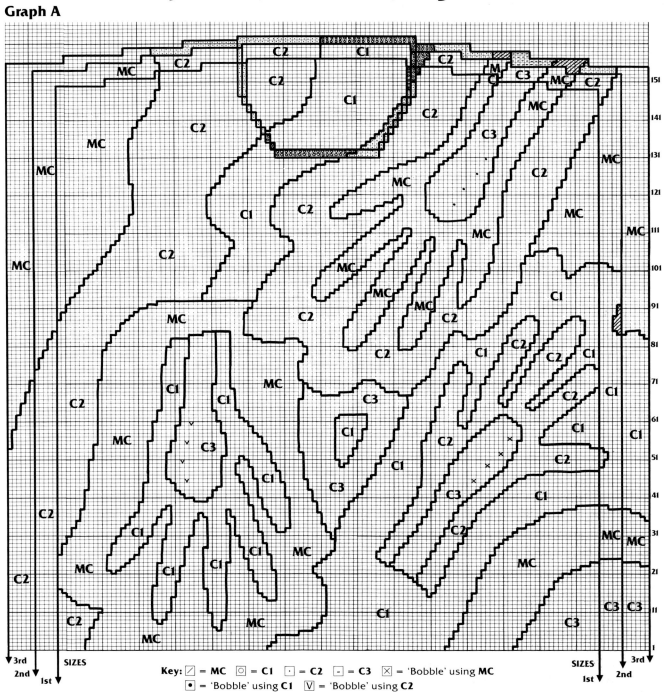

Key: ⊘ = MC   ⊙ = C1   · = C2   - = C3   ⊠ = 'Bobble' using **MC**
⊡ = 'Bobble' using **C1**   Ⓥ = 'Bobble' using **C2**

Maratjara - Many Hands

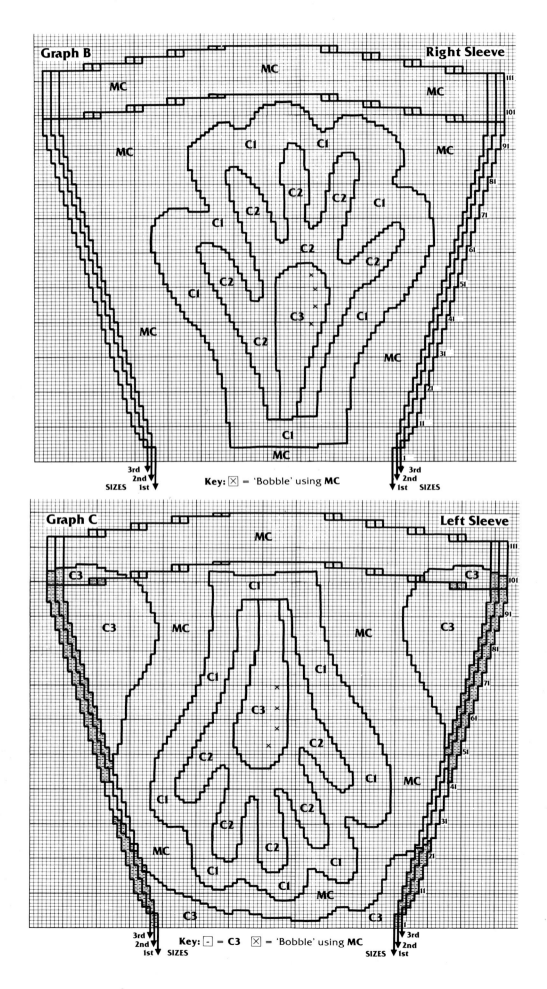

Graph B   **Right Sleeve**

Key: ⊠ = 'Bobble' using **MC**

Graph C   **Left Sleeve**

Key: ⊡ = **C3**   ⊠ = 'Bobble' using **MC**

Didjeridoo Player

Didjeridoo Player

'This instrument comes from north of my country. My people make music by clapping hands and stamping feet, and by using tapping sticks or tapping two boomerangs together.'

The didjeridoo comes from northern Australia, but is now used throughout Aboriginal Australia. It is a major symbol of Aboriginal culture, and its distinctive droning sound often appears on film and television soundtracks. Here Deaggidditt has incorporated it with parallel lines which signify the tracks of the travelling ancestors.

Note: Before commencing the garment it is essential to check your tension (see below).

		S	M	L
To Fit	CM	76-81	86-91	97-102
Bust/Chest	INS	30-32	34-36	38-40
Actual	CM	106	116	127
Measurement	INS	42	46	50
Length to Back	CM	64	65	66
Neck (approx)	INS	25	25½	26
Sleeve Seam				
Women (approx)	CM	43	43	43
	INS	17	17	17
Men (approx)	CM	48	48	48
	INS	19	19	19

Note: This is a loose-fitting garment.

Materials

Cleckheaton 5 Ply Machine Wash 50 g (2 oz) balls **or equivalent yarn to give stated tension.**

	S	M	L
MC (Black)	8	8	9
C (White)	4	4	5

Note: You may require an extra ball of MC for men's sizes.

1 pair each 3.75 mm (No. 9), 3 mm (No. 11), and 1 set of 3 mm (No. 11) knitting needles, or **the required size to give correct tension**; 2 stitch holders; bobbins.

Tension

This garment has been designed at a tension of 26 sts to 10 cm (4 ins) over st st, using 3.75 mm (No. 9) needles.

Note: When working from Graph for Back, read odd numbered rows (knit rows) from left to right, and even numbered rows (purl rows) from right to left.
When working from Graph for Front and Right Sleeve, read odd numbered rows (knit rows) from right to left, and even numbered rows (purl rows) from left to right.

Front

Using 3 mm (No. 11) needles and MC, cast on 123 (137, 151) sts.
1st Row: K2, *P1, K1, rep from * to last st, K1.
2nd Row: K1, *P1, K1, rep from * to end.
Rep 1st and 2nd rows until band measures 8 cm (3 ins) from beg, ending with a 2nd row and inc 16 sts evenly across last row. 139 (153, 167) sts.
Change to 3.75 mm (No. 9) needles and beg patt. ** Work rows 1 to 166 inclusive from Graph A.

Shape neck

Keeping Graph correct,
Next Row: K55 (62, 69), **turn.**
Dec 1 st at left neck edge in alt rows 7 (8, 9) times 48 (54, 60) sts. Work 5 (5, 7) rows.

Shape shoulder

Cast off 12 (14, 15) sts at beg of next row and foll alt row, then 12 (13, 15) sts at beg of foll alt row. Work 1 row. Cast off. Slip next 29 sts onto a stitch holder and leave. Join yarn to rem sts and complete right hand side of neck to correspond with left side.

Back

Work as for Front to **. Work rows 1 to 186 (188, 192) inclusive from Graph A, noting to work C sections in MC where indicated on shaded section of graph.

Shape shoulders

Cast off 12 (14, 15) sts at beg of next 6 (4, 6) rows, then 12 (13, 15) sts at beg of foll 2 (4, 2) rows. Leave rem 43 (45, 47) sts on a stitch holder.

Left sleeve

Using 3 mm (No. 11) needles and MC, cast on 51 (53, 57) sts. Work 8 cm (3 ins) in rib as for lower band of Front, ending with a 2nd row and inc 14 sts evenly across last row. 65 (67, 71) sts. Change to 3.75 mm (No. 9) needles and beg patt. *** Cont in stripes of 10 rows MC and 10 rows C throughout (beg with 10 rows MC), **at same time** inc 1 st at each end of 3rd and foll 4th rows until there are 111 (119, 125) sts, **1st and 2nd Sizes Only** — cont inc in foll 6th row/s until there are 117 (121) sts, **All Sizes** — thus completing 9 (9, 7) rows in MC. Using MC throughout remainder of Sleeve, inc 1 st at each end of 6th (6th, 4th) row, **3rd Size Only** — then in foll 4th row. 119 (123, 129) sts. Work 5 rows for **Women**, or 23 rows for **Men.**

Shape top

Cast off 12 sts at beg of next 10 rows. Cast off rem sts.

Right sleeve

Work as for Left Sleeve to ***. Cont in MC, inc 1 st at each end of 3rd row and foll 4th rows until there are 95 (97, 101) sts. Work 1 row. Work rows 1 to 50 inclusive from Graph B, **at same time** inc 1 st at each end of 3rd and foll 4th rows until there are 111 (119, 125) sts, **1st and 2nd Sizes Only** — cont inc in foll 6th row/s until there are 117 (121) sts. Using C, work 10 rows for **Women**, or 28 rows for **Men, at same time** inc 1 st at each end of 5th (5th, next) row, **3rd Size Only** — and foll 4th row. 119 (123, 129) sts.

Shape top

Complete as for Left Sleeve.

Neckband

Using back-stitch join shoulder seams. With right side facing, using set of 3 mm (No. 11) needles and C, knit up 108 (114, 120) sts evenly around neck edge, including sts from stitch holders.
1st Round: *K1, P1, rep from * to end.
Rep 1st round until band measures 3 cm (1½ ins) from beg. Cast off **loosely** in rib.

To make up

Using back-stitch, sew in Sleeves placing centre top of Sleeve to shoulder seam. Join side and Sleeve seams.

Didjeridoo Player

Graph A

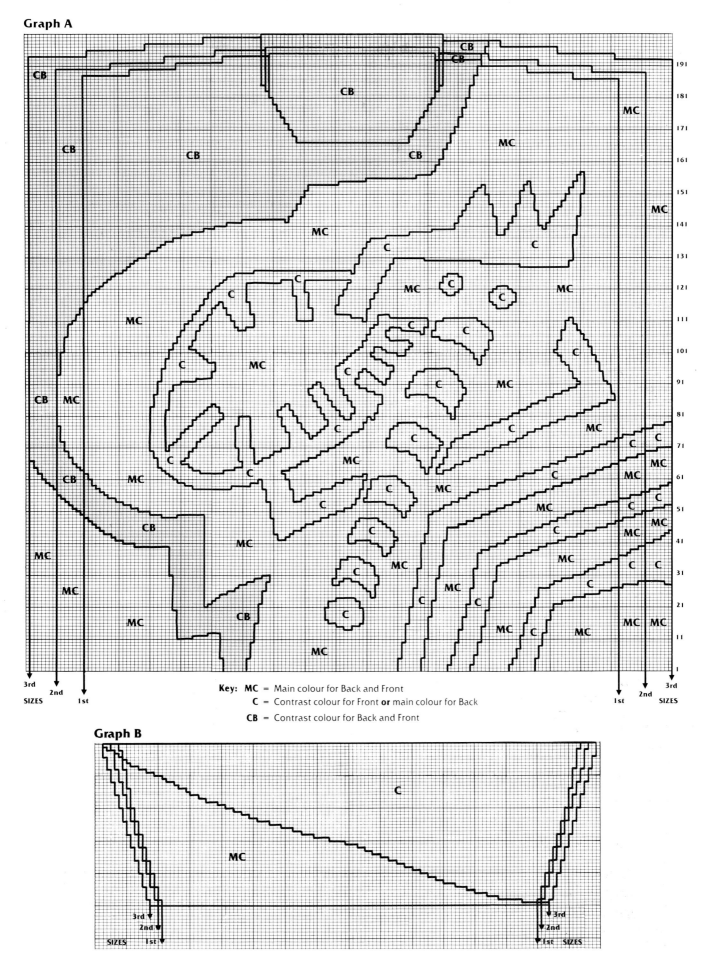

Key: **MC** = Main colour for Back and Front
C = Contrast colour for Front **or** main colour for Back
CB = Contrast colour for Back and Front

Graph B

Marlu - Kangaroo

Marlu - Kangaroo

The kangaroo in this design has the alert eye of a hunted animal. Depicted here in black, it is surrounded by the red of the central Australian earth and the lines and spaces of Aboriginal country.

Note: Before commencing the garment it is essential to check your tension (see below).

		S	M	L
To Fit	CM	76-81	86-91	97-102
Bust/Chest	INS	30-32	34-36	38-40
Actual	CM	106	116	127
Measurement	INS	42	46	50
Length to Back	CM	64	65	66
Neck (approx)	INS	25	25½	26
Sleeve Seam				
Women (approx)	CM	43	43	43
	INS	17	17	17
Men (approx)	CM	48	48	48
	INS	19	19	19

Note: This is a loose-fitting garment.

Materials

Cleckheaton 8 Ply Machine Wash 50 g (2 oz) balls **or equivalent yarn to give stated tension.**

	S	M	L
MC (Blue)	6	6	7
C1 (Red)	5	6	6
C2 (Black)	3	4	4
C3 (Jade)	2	2	2
C4 (White)	Small Quantity		

Note: You may require an extra ball of MC for men's sizes.
1 pair each 4 mm (No. 8), 3.25 mm (No. 10), and 1 set of 3.25 mm (No. 10) knitting needles, or **the required size to give correct tension**; 2 stitch holders; bobbins.

Tension

This garment has been designed at a tension of 22 sts to 10 cm (4 ins) over st st, using 4 mm (No. 8) needles.

Note: When working from Graph B for Back, read odd numbered rows (knit rows) from left to right, and even numbered rows (purl rows) from right to left. When working from Graph B for Front, Graphs C and D for Sleeves, and Graph A for top of Back, read odd numbered rows (knit rows) from right to left, and even numbered rows (purl rows) from left to right.

Back

Using 3.25 mm (No. 10) needles cast on 20 (25, 31) sts in C3, 8 sts in C2, and 75 (80, 86) sts in C1. 103 (113, 125) sts.
Keeping colours correct, throughout band:
1st Row: K2, *P1, K1, rep from * to last st, K1.
2nd Row: K1, *P1, K1, rep from * to end.
Rep 1st and 2nd rows until band measures 8 cm (3 ins) from beg, ending with a 2nd row and inc 16 sts evenly across last row (inc 12 sts in C1, 1 st in C2, and 3 sts in C3). 119 (129, 141) sts.
Change to 4 mm (No. 8) needles and beg patt.**
Take care to follow **separate reading directions** for Graphs A and B.
Work rows 1 to 138 inclusive from Graph B, **omitting** Kangaroo (using C1 to replace Kangaroo) and omitting C2 in rows 136 to 138 inclusive as indicated on Graph B.
Work rows 1 to 22 (24, 28) inclusive from Graph A.

Shape shoulders

Keeping Graph correct, cast off 11 (12, 13) sts at beg of next 4 (4, 6) rows, then 10 (11, 12) sts at beg of foll 4 (4, 2) rows.
Leave rem 35 (37, 39) sts on a stitch holder.

Front

Work as for Back to **, reversing colours in lower band. Work rows 1 to 142 (142, 144) inclusive from Graph B.

Shape neck

Keeping Graph correct,
Next Row: K48 (53, 58), **turn**.
Dec 1 st at left neck edge in alt rows 6 (7, 7) times. 42 (46, 51) sts. Work 5 (5, 7) rows.

Shape shoulder

Cast off 11 (12, 13) sts at beg of next row and foll alt row, then 10 (11, 13) sts at beg of foll alt row.
Work 1 row. Cast off. Slip next 23 (23, 25) sts onto a stitch holder and leave. Join yarn to rem sts at right neck edge and complete to correspond with left side.

Left sleeve (worked sideways)

Using 4 mm (No. 8) needles and MC, cast on 8 sts for **Women**, or 16 sts for **Men**.
Keeping Graph C correct, cast on 4 sts at beg of 3rd and foll alt row 18 (15, 12) times in all, **2nd and 3rd Sizes Only** — then cast on 3 sts at beg of alt rows (4, 8) times. Work 61 rows from Graph C.
Cast off 4 (3, 3) sts at beg of next row and foll alt rows 18 (4, 8) times, **2nd and 3rd Sizes Only** — then cast off 4 sts at beg of alt rows (15, 12) times. Work 1 row.
Cast off.

Right sleeve (worked sideways)

Keeping Graph D correct, complete to correspond with Left Sleeve, reversing shapings as indicated.

Neckband

Using back-stitch, join shoulder seams.
With right side facing, using set of 3.25 mm (No. 10) needles and MC, knit up 92 (98, 106) sts evenly around neck edge, including sts from stitch holders.
1st Round: *K1, P1, rep from * to end. Rep 1st round 9 times. Cast off **loosely** in rib.

Wristbands (make 2)

Using 3.25 mm (No. 10) needles and MC for Left Sleeve or C3 for Right Sleeve, cast on 43 (45, 47) sts. Work in rib as for lower band of Back until band measures 9 cm (3¾ ins) from beg, ending with a 2nd row. Cast off **loosely** in rib.

To make up

Using back-stitch, sew in Sleeves placing centre top of Sleeve to shoulder seam. Join side and Sleeve seams. Join Wristband seams and sew Wristbands in position, gathering Sleeves to fit.

Marlu - Kangaroo

Graph A

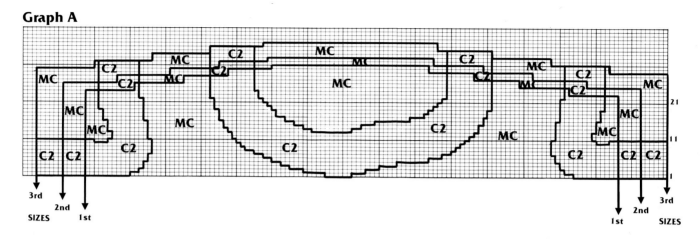

Graph B

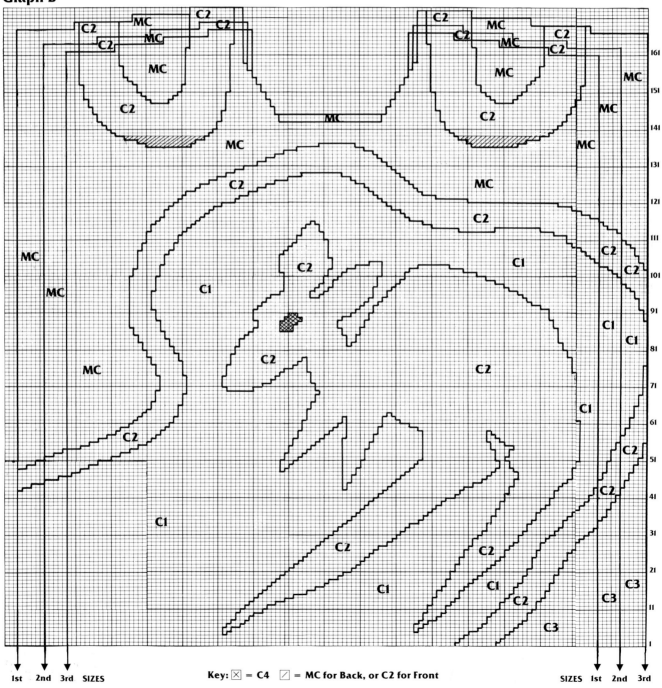

Key: ☒ = C4   ☑ = MC for Back, or C2 for Front

Marlu - Kangaroo

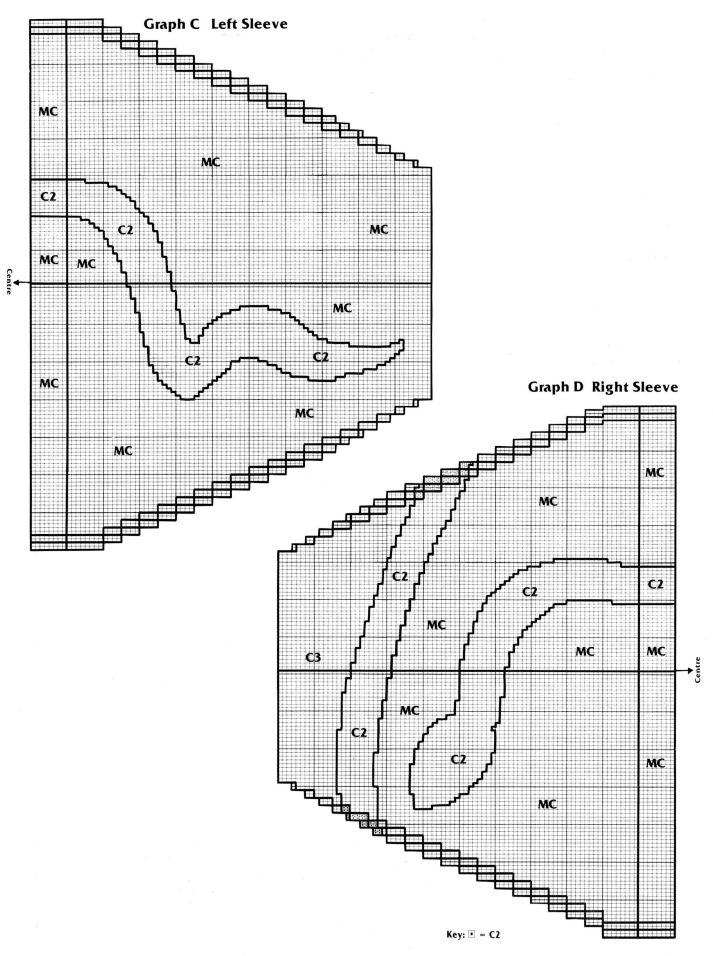

Graph C Left Sleeve

Centre

Graph D Right Sleeve

Centre

Key: ⊡ = C2

Mara - Hand

Mara - Hand

The blueish-grey eggs of the emu have a kind of stippled surface. In fairly recent times Aboriginal artists have carved designs into these eggs combining different motifs in the same way that Deaggidditt has combined the hand motif with that of the emu chick.

Note: Before commencing the garment it is essential to check your tension (see below).

		S	M	L
To Fit	CM	76-81	86-91	97-102
Bust/Chest	INS	30-32	34-36	38-40
Actual	CM	106	116	127
Measurement	INS	42	46	50
Length to Back	CM	64	65	66
Neck (approx)	INS	25	25½	26
Sleeve Seam				
Women (approx)	CM	46	46	46
	INS	18	18	18
Men (approx)	CM	50	50	50
	INS	19½	19½	19½

Note: This is a loose-fitting garment.

Materials

Cleckheaton Natural 8 Ply 50 g (2 oz) balls or equivalent yarn to give stated tension.

	S	M	L
MC (Khaki)	8	9	10
C1 (Rust)	3	3	3
C2 (Sand)	2	2	2
C3 (Black)	3	3	3
C4 (Brown)	3	3	3

Note: You may require an extra ball of MC for men's sizes.
1 pair each 4 mm (No. 8) and 3.25 mm (No. 10) knitting needles, or **the required size to give correct tension**; 1 stitch holder; bobbins; 8 buttons.

Tension

This garment has been designed at a tension of 22 sts to 10 cm (4 ins) over st st, using 4 mm (No. 8) needles.

Abbreviation

'Bobble' = (K1, P1, K1, P1) in next st, **turn**, P4, **turn**, K4, **turn**, P4, **turn**, K4, pass 2nd, 3rd and 4th sts over first st.

Note: When working from Graph for Back, read odd numbered rows (knit rows) from left to right, and even numbered rows (purl rows) from right to left. When working from Graph for Front, read odd numbered rows from right to left, and even numbered from left to right.

Back

Using 3.25 mm (No. 10) needles and MC, cast on 109 (119, 131) sts.
1st Row: K2, *P1, K1, rep from * to last st, K1.
2nd Row: K1, *P1, K1, rep from * to end.
Rep 1st and 2nd rows until band measures 8 cm (3 ins) from beg, ending with a 2nd row and inc 10 sts evenly across last row. 119 (129, 141) sts.
Change to 4 mm (No. 8) needles and beg patt. Work rows 1 to 160 (162, 166) inclusive from Graph A.

Shape shoulders

Keeping Graph correct, cast off 11 (12, 13) sts at beg of next 4 (4, 6) rows, then 10 (11, 12) sts at beg of foll 4 (4, 2) rows. Leave rem 35 (37, 39) sts on a stitch holder.

Left front

Using 3.25 mm (No. 10) needles and MC, cast on 55 (61, 67) sts. Work in rib as for lower band of Back until band measures 8 cm (3 ins) from beg, ending with a 2nd row, and inc 4 (3, 3) sts evenly across last row. 59 (64, 70) sts.
Change to 4 mm (No. 8) needles and beg patt. Work rows 1 to 143 (143, 145) inclusive from Graph A as indicated for Left Front.

Shape neck

Keeping Graph correct, cast off 11 (11, 12) sts at beg of next row. Dec 1 st at neck edge in next and foll alt rows 6 (7, 7) times in all. 42 (46, 51) sts. Work 5 (5, 7) rows.

Shape shoulder

Cast off 11 (12, 13) sts at beg of next row and foll alt row, then 10 (11, 13) sts at beg of foll alt row. Work 1 row. Cast off.

Right front

Work to correspond with Left Front, following Graph A for Right Front.

Left sleeve (worked sideways)

Using 4 mm (No. 8) needles and MC, cast on 16 sts. Keeping Graph B correct, cast on 4 sts at beg of 3rd and foll alt rows 18 (15, 12) times in all, **2nd and 3rd Sizes Only** — then cast on 3 sts at beg of foll alt rows 4 (8) times. Work 29 rows from Graph.
Rep last 2 rows 0 (2, 4) times, keeping colours correct as placed. Work next 30 rows from Graph.
Cast off 4 (3, 3) sts at beg of next row and foll alt rows 18 (4, 8) times, **2nd and 3rd Sizes Only** — then cast off 4 sts at beg of alt rows (15, 12) times. On rem 16 sts work 3 rows. Cast off.

Right sleeve (worked sideways)

Keeping Graph C correct, work to correspond with Left Sleeve noting no rows are repeated.

Buttonhole bands

Right front band for women, left front band for men

Using 3.25 mm (No. 10) needles and MC, cast on 11 sts. Work 4 rows rib as for lower band of Back.
5th Row: Rib 4, yfwd, K2tog, rib 3.
Work 25 rows rib. Rep last 26 rows 6 times more, then first 22 of these 26 rows once. 7 buttonholes. Leave sts on a spare needle.

Left front band for women, right front band for men

Work as for other Front Band omitting buttonholes.

Mara - Hand

Graph A

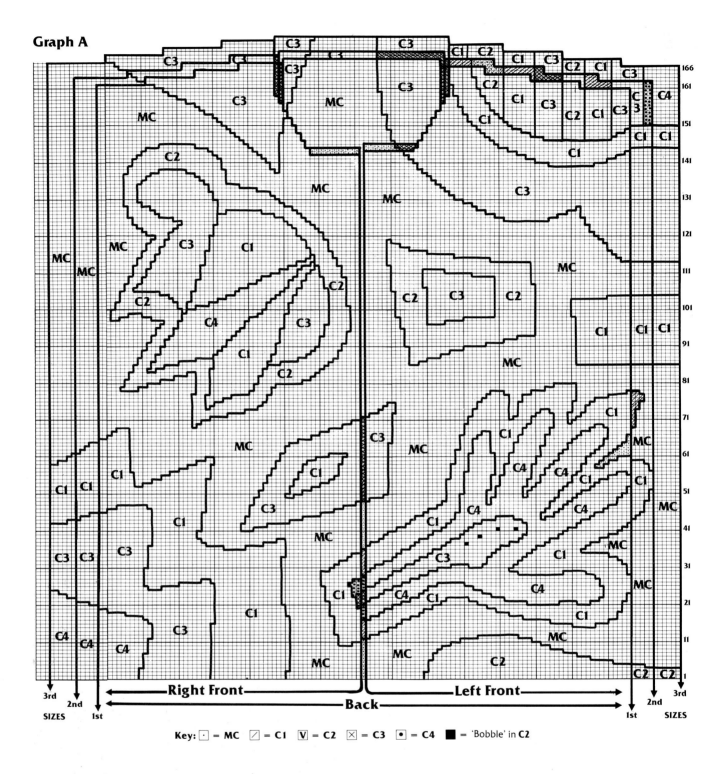

Key: · = MC   ╱ = C1   V = C2   ⊠ = C3   • = C4   ■ = 'Bobble' in C2

Neckband

Using back-stitch, join shoulder seams. With right side facing, using 3.25 mm (No. 10) needles and MC, rib across Right Front Band sts, knit up 89 (95, 103) sts evenly around neck edge, including sts from stitch holder, then rib across Left Front Band sts. 111 (117, 125) sts. Work 3 rows rib.

Women: 4th Row Rib 4, yfwd, K2tog, rib to end.

Men: 4th Row Rib to last five sts, yfwd, K2tog, rib 3.

All sizes work 5 rows rib. Cast off **loosely** in rib.

Wristbands

Using 3.25 mm (No. 10) needles and MC, cast on 45 (47, 49) sts. Work in rib as for lower band of Back until band measures 3.5 cm (1½ ins) from beg for **Women**, or 7.5 cm (3 ins) from beg for **Men**, ending with a 2nd row. Cast off **loosely** in rib.

To make up

Using back-stitch, sew in Sleeves placing centre top of Sleeve to shoulder seam. Join side and Sleeve seams. Sew Front Bands in position stretching slightly to fit. Sew on buttons. Join Wristband seams and sew Wristbands in position, gathering Sleeves to fit.

Mara - Hand

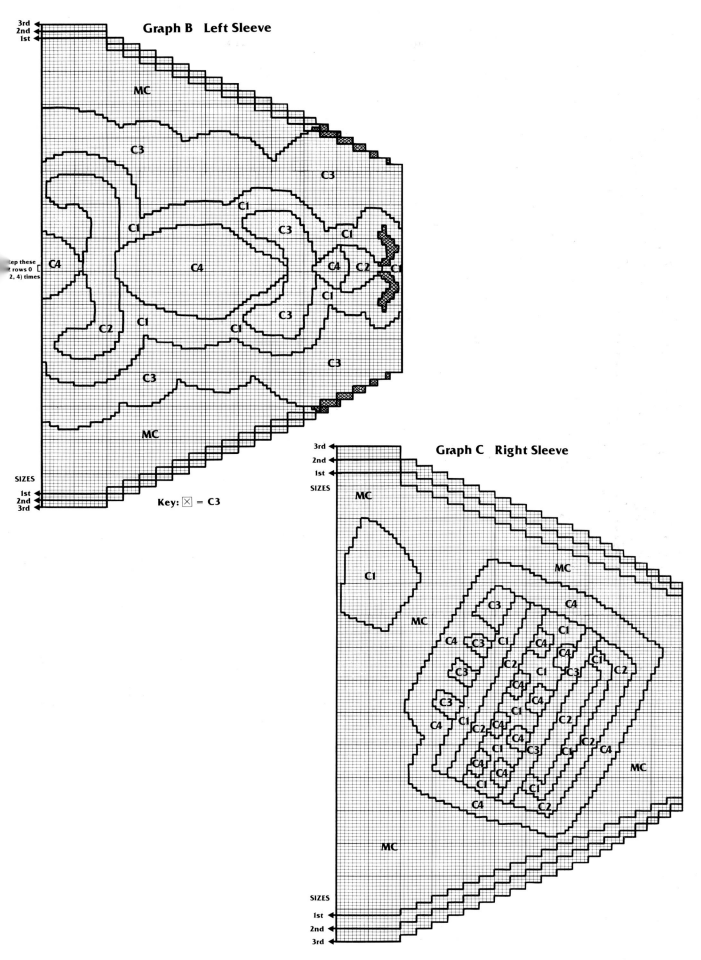

Graph B   Left Sleeve

Key: ☒ = C3

Graph C   Right Sleeve

GRINDING STONES AND TREE BARK

DORIS GINGINGARA

Doris Gingingara was born in 1946 at Maningrida, an Aboriginal community town in Arnhem Land in the Northern Territory. Her tribal group is *Barada* and she spent her childhood in the traditional way with her parents and her tribe, hunting and gathering. Twice she was taken by the *Mimi* spirits and put into a tree to be taught about basket and net making. *Mimi* are important figures in the cultures of Arnhem Land, and are often depicted in bark paintings as long thin humans. They can only be glimpsed in dreams or the half-light, and make themselves fully present only to 'doctors', the clever people of the tribe. Doris's capture indicates the importance of these spirits in the cultural life of Aborigines. Knowledge is not so much achieved by individuals as conceived in the Dreaming and passed on from generation to generation. This is how she tells the story:

Djunuwiny *is a sacred place to me, this is the place where spirits came to get me when I was a little girl. My parents were looking for me and call my name. When spirits heard this they put me on the beach so my parents could see me. Dad got some green ants and put them around me so I could wake up, then I was all right and my parents did not worry anymore when I went a little bit far way because they knew spirits were looking after me.*

Later she went to school in Darwin, living there and going back to visit her family at Maningrida during the holidays.

After cyclone Tracy hit Darwin in 1974, Doris moved to Perth, Geraldton and finally Mount Magnet in Western Australia, where she now lives with her French-born husband Danny. It was after moving to Mount Magnet that she started drawing, initially for fun and to pass the time. Her inspiration is from everyday life, her childhood in Arnhem Land, and from things she sees around her, mostly to do with nature — plants, flowers, rocks and animals. Doris has visited France several times, but her work still draws on the countryside around Mount Magnet.

D·GINGINGARA

Leaves and Tracks

Leaves and Tracks

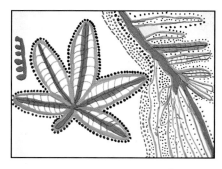

'When I want to find designs for my work, I often wander down by the creek. There, in the tiny little details like leaves and the tracks of insects, I can see the patterns I will use in my art.'

Aboriginal people survive in their land by being able to read the country. Even small things like leaves in the mud or the tracks of beetles can tell a story. Beetle tracks may indicate a search for food, and the 'increase' of that animal in a particular season may mean something else, for example that the food gatherer should be on the lookout for fat bream in the river.

Note: Before commencing the garment it is essential to check your tension (see below).

		S	M	L
To Fit	CM	76-81	86-91	97-102
Bust/Chest	INS	30-32	34-36	38-40
Actual	CM	99	109	120
Measurement	INS	39	43	47
Length to Back	CM	63	64	65
Neck	INS	25	25	25½

Materials

Cleckheaton Natural 8 Ply 50 g (2 oz) balls or equivalent yarn to give stated tension.

	S	M	L
MC (Rust)	7	8	9
C1 (Blue)	1	1	1
C2 (Brown)	1	1	1
C3 (Black)	1	1	1

1 pair each 4 mm (No. 8), 3.25 mm (No. 10), and 1 set of 3.25 mm (No. 10) knitting needles, or **the required size to give correct tension**; 1 stitch holder; bobbins.

Tension

This garment has been designed at a tension of 22 sts to 10 cm (4 ins) over st st, using 4 mm (No. 8) needles.

Abbreviations

'Bobble' = (K1, P1, K1, P1) in next st, **turn**, P4, **turn**, K4, **turn**, P4, **turn**, pass 1st, 2nd and 3rd sts over 4th st.

Back

Using 3.25 mm (No. 10) needles and MC, cast on 97 (107, 119) sts.
1st Row: K2, *P1, K1, rep from * to last st, K1.
2nd Row: K1, *P1, K1, rep from * to end.
Rep 1st and 2nd rows until band measures 8 cm (3 ins) from beg, ending with a 2nd row and inc 14 sts evenly across last row. 111 (121, 133) sts. Change to 4 mm (No. 8) needles. ** Work 86 rows st st (1 row K, 1 row P).

Shape armholes

Cast off 7 (9, 10) sts at beg of next 2 rows. Dec 1 st at each end of next row and foll alt rows until 83 (87, 93) sts rem. Work 47 rows.

Shape shoulders

Cast off 8 (8, 9) sts at beg of next 4 rows, then 8 (9, 9) sts at beg of foll 2 rows. Leave rem 35 (37, 39) sts on a stitch holder.

Front

Work as for Back to **. Work rows 1 to 76 inclusive from Graph.

Divide for 'V' neck
Left side of neck

Keeping Graph correct,
Next Row: 55 (60, 66), **turn**. Dec 1 st at neck edge in alt rows 4 times. 51 (56, 62) sts. Work 1 row.

Shape armhole

Keeping Graph correct,
Next Row: cast off 7 (9, 10) sts, K to last 2 sts, K2tog. Cont on last 43 (46, 51) sts and dec 1 st at armhole edge in alt rows 7 (8, 10) times, **at same time** dec 1 st at neck edge in 4th rows 12 (13, 14) times. 24 (25, 27) sts. Work 13 (11, 11) rows.

Shape shoulder

Cast off 8 (8, 9) sts at beg of next row and foll alt row. Work 1 row. Cast off.

Right side of neck

Slip next st on to a coloured thread and leave (centre st). Join yarn to rem sts at right neck edge, and keeping Graph correct, complete to correspond with left hand side.

Neckband

Using back-stitch, join shoulder seams. With right side facing, using set of 3.25 mm (No. 10) needles and MC, beg at left shoulder seam and knit up 64 (66, 70) sts evenly along left side of neck, knit st from coloured thread (centre st), knit up 64 (66, 70) sts evenly along right side of neck, and knit across sts from back neck stitch holder. 164 (170, 180) sts.

1st Round: *K1, P1, rep from * to end.
2nd Round: Rib to within 2 sts of centre st, ybk sl 1, K1, psso, K1 (centre st), K2tog, rib to end.
3rd Round: Rib to within 2 sts of centre st, P2togtbl, K1, P2tog, rib to end. Rep 2nd and 3rd rounds 4 times. Cast off **loosely** in rib.

Armbands

With right side facing, using 3.25 mm (No. 10) needles and MC, knit up 123 (127, 135) sts evenly along armhole edge. Work 9 rows rib as for lower band of Back, beg with a 2nd row. Cast off **loosely** in rib.

To make up

Using back-stitch, join side and Armband seams. If desired, veins of leaf can be embroidered on in stem stitch.

Leaves and Tracks

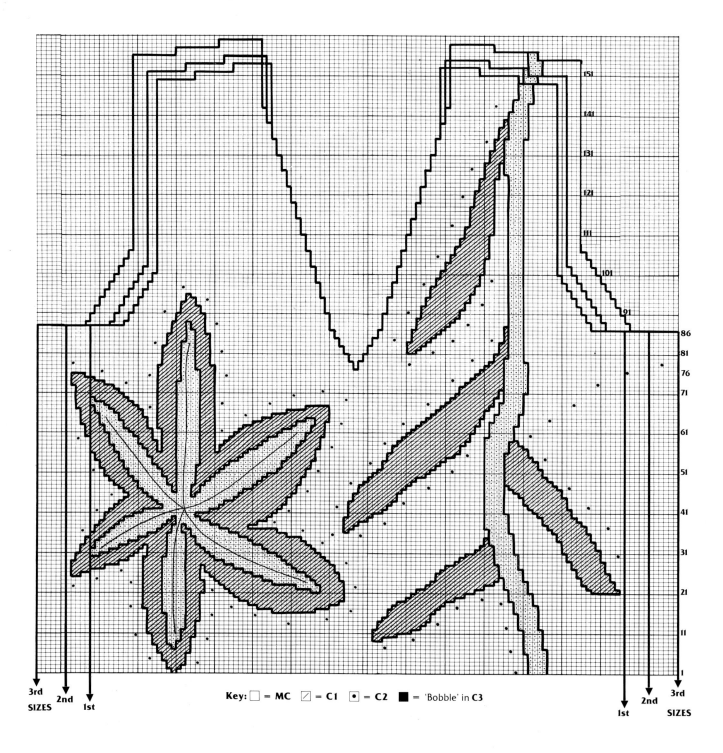

Key: ☐ = MC   ▨ = C1   ⊡ = C2   ■ = 'Bobble' in C3

3rd SIZES   2nd   1st

1st   2nd   3rd SIZES

84

Batjikala - Long Pipe

Batjikala - Long Pipe

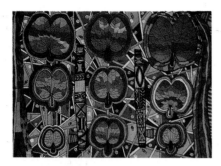

'These pipes can be smoked either by men or women, but are always made by the men. Each family has their own tree from which they get the wood for making the pipes.'

The smoking pipes are particular to each family. As well as having their own tree, they decorate the pipes with designs that belong only to their own family group. They are, in some ways, an Aboriginal form of writing, since each carries a different message.

Note: Before commencing the garment it is essential to check your tension (see below).

		S	M	L
To Fit	CM	76-81	86-91	97-102
Bust/Chest	INS	30-32	34-36	38-40
Actual	CM	106	116	127
Measurement	INS	42	46	50
Length to Back	CM	68	69	70
Neck (approx)	INS	27	27	27½
Sleeve Seam				
Women (approx)	CM	43	43	43
	INS	17	17	17
Men (approx)	CM	48	48	48
	INS	19	19	19

Note: This is a loose-fitting garment.

Materials

Cleckheaton Natural 8 Ply 50 g (2 oz) balls or equivalent yarn to give stated tension.

	S	M	L
MC (Grey)	11	12	13
C1 (Dark Brown)	2	2	2
C2 (Rust)	1	1	1
C3 (Black)	1	1	1

Note: You may require an extra ball of MC for men's sizes.
1 pair each 4 mm (No. 8) and 3.25 mm (No.10) knitting needles or, **the required size to give correct tension;**
1 stitch holder; bobbins; 8 buttons.

Tension

This garment has been designed at a tension of 22 sts to 10 cm (4 ins) over st st, using 4 mm (No. 8) needles.

Back

Using 3.25 mm (No. 10) needles and MC, cast on 105 (115, 127) sts.
1st Row: K2, *P1, K1, rep from * to last st, K1.

2nd Row: K1, *P1, K1, rep from * to end.
Rep 1st and 2nd rows until band measures 6 cm (2½ ins) from beg, ending with a 2nd row and inc 13 sts evenly across last row. 118 (128, 140) sts.
Change to 4 mm (No. 8) needles. Work 174 (176, 178) rows st st (1 row K, 1 row P).

Shape shoulders

Cast off 10 (11, 13) sts at beg of next 6 rows, then 11 (12, 11) sts at beg of foll 2 rows. Leave rem 36 (38, 40) sts on a stitch holder.

Left front

Using 3.25 mm (No. 10) needles and MC, cast on 53 (59, 65) sts. Work in rib as for lower band of Back, until band measures 6 cm (2½ ins) from beg, ending with a 2nd row and inc 6 (5, 5) sts evenly across last row. 59 (64, 70) sts.
Change to 4 mm (No. 8) needles.
Work rows 1 to 157 inclusive from Graph for Left Front.

Shape neck

Keeping Graph correct, cast off 9 sts at beg of next row. Dec 1 st at neck edge in **every** row until 41 (45, 50) sts rem. Work 7 (6, 5) rows, thus completing Graph. Using MC, work 0 (2, 4) rows st st.

Shape shoulder

Cast off 10 (11, 13) sts at beg of next and foll alt rows 3 times in all. Work 1 row. Cast off.

Right front

Work to correspond with Left Front, following Graph as indicated for Right Front.

Sleeves

Using 3.25 mm (No.10) needles and MC, cast on 45 (47, 49) sts.
Work in rib as for lower band of Back until band measures 6 cm (2½ ins) from beg, ending with a 2nd row and inc 15 sts evenly across last row. 60 (62, 64) sts.
Change to 4 mm (No. 8) needles. Cont in st st inc 1 st at each end of 3rd row and foll 4th rows until there are 86 (94, 102) sts, then in foll 6th rows until there are 102 (106, 110) sts.
Cont without shaping until side edge measures 43 cm (17 ins) for **Women**, or 48 cm (19 ins) **Men**, from beg, ending with a purl row.

Shape top

Cast off 10 sts at beg of next 8 rows.
Cast off rem sts.

Buttonhole bands

Right front band for women, left front band for men

Using 3.25 mm (No. 10) needles and MC, cast on 11 sts.
1st Row: K2, (P1, K1) 4 times, K1.

2nd Row: (K1, P1) 5 times, K1.
3rd Row: Rib 5, cast off 2 sts, rib 4.
4th Row: Rib 4, cast on 2 sts, rib 5.
Work 24 rows rib. Rep last 26 rows 5 times, then 3rd and 4th rows once. 7 Buttonholes. Work 22 rows rib. ** Break off yarn, leave sts on a spare needle.

Left front band for women, right front band for men

Work as for other Front Band omitting buttonholes, to **. Do not break off yarn. Leave sts on needle.

Neckband

Using back-stitch, join shoulder seams. With right side facing, using 3.25 mm (No. 10) needles and MC, rib across 11 sts on Right Front Band, knit up 93 (99, 105) sts evenly around neck edge, including sts from back neck stitch holder, then rib across Left Front Band sts. 115 (121, 127) sts. Work 9 rows rib as for lower band of Back, beg with a 2nd row of rib and working a buttonhole (as before) in 2nd and 3rd rows of neckband. Cast off **loosely** in rib.

To make up

Using back-stitch, sew in Sleeves placing centre top of Sleeve to shoulder seam. Join side and Sleeve seams. Sew Front Bands in position stretching slightly to fit. Sew on buttons.

Batjikala - Long Pipe

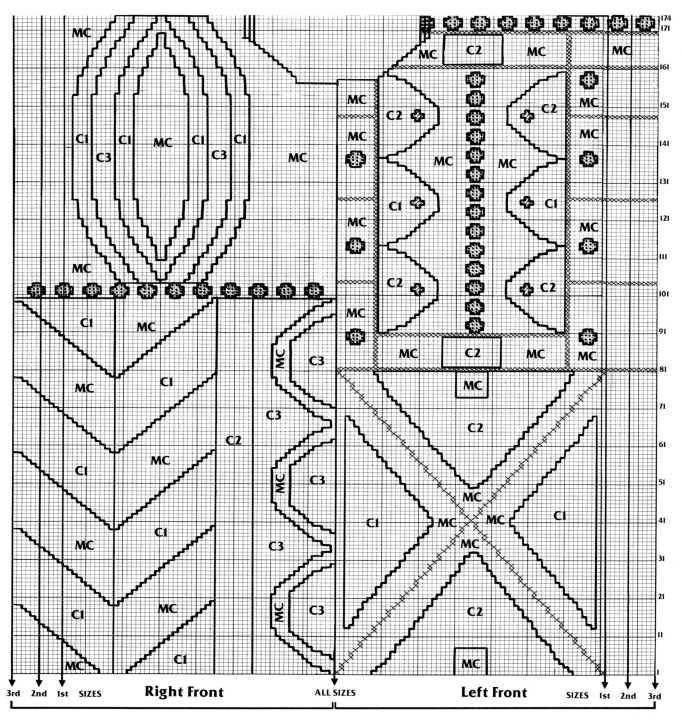

Key: ⧄ = MC   ⊡ = C1   ⊠ = C3

Barramundi

Barramundi

'Barramundi is one of the favourite foods of Arnhem Land Aborigines. It likes turbulent water, where it feeds on smaller fish, fresh water shrimps, even small snakes. The Aborigines catch it in different ways; trapping and netting, spearing, and putting a narcotic juice in the water which makes the fish easy to catch. A large barramundi is called radjerra.'

This colourful design borrows the traditional technique from northern Australia sometimes called 'X-ray design'. Parts of the insides of the fish are shown, even the gut which has to be removed before eating.

Note: Before commencing the garment it is essential to check your tension (see below).

		S	M	L
To Fit	CM	76-81	86-91	97-102
Bust/Chest	INS	30-32	34-36	38-40
Actual	CM	106	116	127
Measurement	INS	42	46	50
Length to Back	CM	64	64	64
Neck (approx)	INS	25	25½	26
Sleeve Seam				
Women (approx)	CM	43	43	43
	INS	17	17	17
Men (approx)	CM	48	48	48
	INS	19	19	19

Note: This is a loose-fitting garment.

Materials

Cleckheaton 8 Ply Machine Wash 50 g (2 oz) balls **or equivalent yarn to give stated tension.**

	S	M	L
MC (Aqua)	11	12	13
C1 (Blue)	1	1	1
C2 (Dark Grey)	1	1	1
C3 (Light Grey)	1	1	1
C4 (Mauve)	1	1	1
C5 (Yellow)	1	1	1
C6 (Coral)	1	1	1
C7 (Black)	Small Quantity		

Note: You may require an extra ball of MC for men's sizes.

1 pair each 4 mm (No. 8) and 3.25 mm (No. 10), and 1 set of 3.25 mm (No. 10) knitting needles, or **the required size to give correct tension;**

2 stitch holders; bobbins.

Tension

This garment has been designed at a tension of 22 sts to 10 cm (4 ins) over st st, using 4 mm (No. 8) needles.

Back

Using 3.25 mm (No. 10) needles and MC, cast on 103 (113, 125) sts.
1st Row: K2, *P1, K1, rep from * to last st, K1.
2nd Row: K1, *P1, K1, rep from * to end.
Rep 1st and 2nd rows until band measures 8 cm (3 ins) from beg, ending with a 2nd row and inc 16 sts evenly across last row. 119 (129, 141) sts.
Change to 4 mm (No. 8) needles and beg patt.** Work 142 rows st st (1 row K, 1 row P). Work rows 1 to 20 inclusive from Graph A.

Shape shoulders

Keeping Graph A correct, cast off 11 (12, 13) sts at beg of next 4 (4, 6) rows, then 10 (11, 12) sts at beg of foll 4 (4, 2) rows. Leave rem 35 (37, 39) sts on a stitch holder.

Front

Work as for Back to **. Work rows 1 to 144 (142, 140) inclusive from Graph B.

Shape neck

Keeping Graph correct,
Next Row: K48 (53, 58), **turn.**
Dec 1 st at left neck edge in alt rows 6 (7, 7) times. Work 5 (5, 7) rows.

Shape shoulder

Cast off 11 (12, 13) sts at beg of next row and foll alt row, then 10 (11, 13) sts at beg of foll alt row. Work 1 row. Cast off. Slip next 23 (23, 25) sts onto a stitch holder and leave. Join yarn to rem sts and complete right hand side of neck to correspond with left side.

Left sleeve (worked sideways)

Using 4 mm (No. 8) needles and MC, cast on 8 sts for **Women** or 16 sts for **Men.** *** Work 2 rows st st, beg where indicated on Graph C. ****Keeping Graph C correct throughout, cast on 4 sts at beg of next row and foll alt rows 18 (15, 12) times in all, **2nd and 3rd Sizes Only** — then 3 sts in foll alt rows (4, 8) times. Work 61 (61, 65) rows from Graph C.
2nd and 3rd Sizes Only — Cast off 3 sts at beg of next and foll alt rows (4, 8) times

in all. Work 1 row. **All Sizes** — Cast off 4 sts at beg of next and foll alt rows 18 (15, 12) times in all. **** Work 1 row. Cast off.

Right sleeve (worked sideways)

Work as for Left Sleeve to ***. Work 3 rows st st. Rep from **** to ****, working from Graph D in place of Graph C. Work 2 rows. Cast off.

Neckband

Using back-stitch, join shoulder seams. With right side facing, using set of 3.25 mm (No. 10) needles and MC, knit up 104 (110, 118) sts evenly around neck edge, including sts from stitch holders.
1st Round: *K1, P1, rep from * to end. Rep 1st round 9 times. Cast off **loosely** in rib.

Wristbands (make 2)

Using 3.25 mm (No. 10) needles and MC, cast on 43 (45, 47) sts. Work in rib as for lower band of Back until band measures 7 cm (2¾ ins) from beg, ending with a 2nd row. Cast off **loosely** in rib.

To make up

Using back-stitch, sew in Sleeves placing centre top of Sleeve to shoulder seam. Join side and Sleeve seams. Join Wristband seams and sew Wristband in position, gathering Sleeves to fit.

Barramundi

Graph A

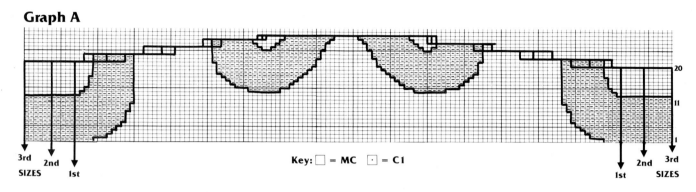

20
11
1

3rd SIZES   2nd   1st

Key: ☐ = MC   ⊡ = C1

1st   2nd   3rd SIZES

Graph B

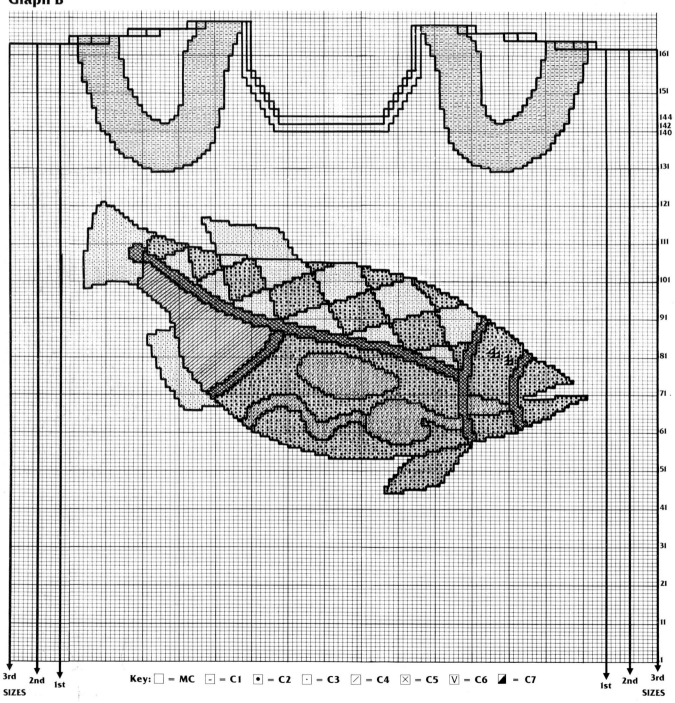

161
151
144
142
140
131
121
111
101
91
81
71
61
51
41
31
21
11
1

3rd SIZES   2nd   1st

Key: ☐ = MC   ⊟ = C1   ⊡ = C2   ⊡ = C3   ⧄ = C4   ⊠ = C5   ⊻ = C6   ◪ = C7

1st   2nd   3rd SIZES

Barramundi

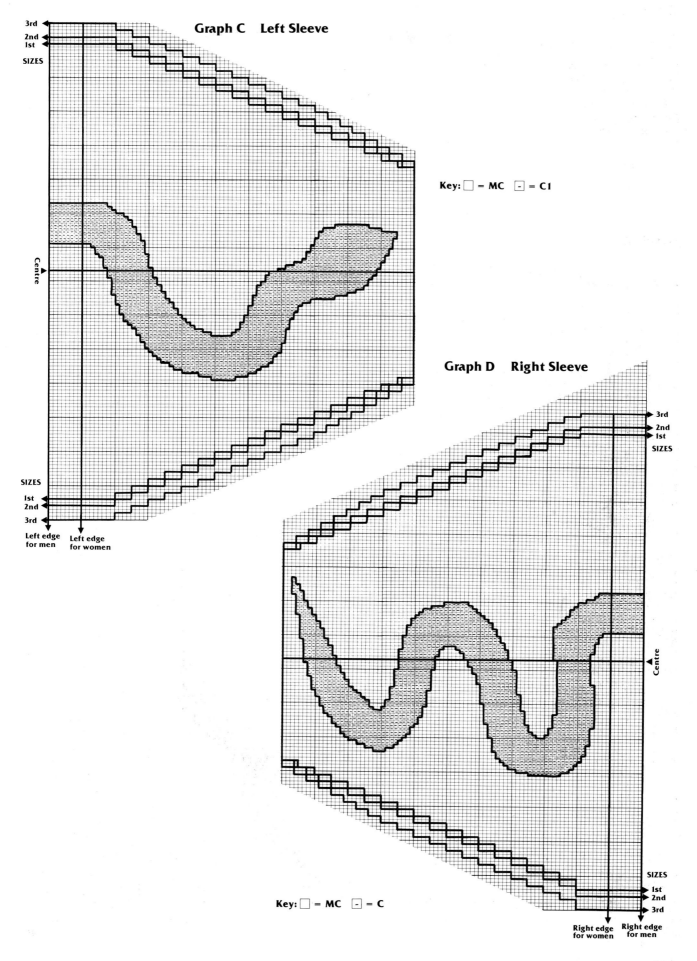

Graph C Left Sleeve

3rd
2nd
1st

SIZES

Key: ☐ = MC - = C1

Centre

SIZES

1st
2nd
3rd

Left edge
for men

Left edge
for women

Graph D Right Sleeve

3rd
2nd
1st

SIZES

Centre

SIZES

1st
2nd
3rd

Right edge
for women

Right edge
for men

Key: ☐ = MC - = C

Djarram - Tree Bark Nets

Djarram - Tree Bark Nets

'Tree bark is used for making string for baskets and fish traps. Only the bark from the roots is used and both men and women make the string and the nets. Those nets are small and are meant to be used by one or two people. They are called djarram. *The name of the tree is* kaluwun. Djarram *is also the name for a spiderweb. The string is called* yatja.*'*

Here Doris Gingingarra is giving us information about the practical use of natural materials. Her design shows us the beauty of the relationship between man-made artifacts and natural materials. In Aboriginal languages, cross-hatching in painting, parallel grooves in wood, dots and other patterns are described by the same word that might be used for spider webs, lines in beach sand or honeycombs.

Note: Before commencing the garment it is essential to check your tension (see below).

		S	M	L
To Fit	CM	76-81	86-91	97-102
Bust/Chest	INS	30-32	34-36	38-40
Actual	CM	106	116	127
Measurement	INS	42	46	50
Length to Back	CM	64	65	66
Neck (approx)	INS	25	25½	26
Sleeve Seam				
Women (approx)	CM	43	43	43
	INS	17	17	17
Men (approx)	CM	48	48	48
	INS	19	19	19

Note: This is a loose-fitting garment.

Materials

Cleckheaton 8 Ply Machine Wash 50 g (2 oz) balls **or equivalent yarn to give stated tension.**

	S	M	L
MC (Cream)	12	13	14
C1 (Navy)	1	1	1
C2 (Bottle)	1	1	1
C3 (Red)	1	1	1
C4 (Rust)	1	1	1

Note: You may require an extra ball of MC for men's sizes.
1 pair each 4 mm (No. 8) and 3.25 mm (No. 10), and 1 set of 3.25 mm (No. 10) knitting needles, or **the required size to give correct tension**; 2 stitch holders; bobbins.

Tension

This garment has been designed at a tension of 22 sts to 10 cm (4 ins) over st st, using 4 mm (No. 8) needles.

Front

Using 3.25 mm (No. 10) needles and MC, cast on 105 (115, 127) sts.
1st Row: K2, *P1, K1, rep from * to last st, K1.
2nd Row: K1, *P1, K1, rep from * to end.
Rep 1st and 2nd rows until band measures 6 cm (2½ ins) from beg, ending with a 2nd row and inc 13 sts evenly across last row. 118 (128, 140) sts.
Change to 4 mm (No. 8) needles.** Work rows 1 to 156 inclusive from Graph.

Shape neck

Keeping Graph correct,
Next Row: K47 (52, 58), **turn.**
Dec 1 st at left neck edge in alt rows 6 (7, 8) times. 41 (45, 50) sts rem. Work 5 rows.

Shape shoulder

Cast off 10 (11, 13) sts at beg of next and foll alt rows 3 times in all. Work 1 row. Cast off. Slip next 24 sts onto a stitch holder and leave. Join yarn to rem sts at right neck edge and complete to correspond with left side of neck.

Back

Work as for Front to **. Using MC, cont in st st (1 row K, 1 row P) until work measures same as Front to shoulder shaping.

Shape shoulders

Cast off 10 (11, 13) sts at beg of next 6 rows, then 11 (12, 11) sts at beg of foll 2 rows. Leave rem 36 (38, 40) sts on a stitch holder.

Sleeves

Using 3.25 mm (No. 10) needles and MC, cast on 45 (47, 49) sts. Work in rib as for lower band of Front until band measures 6 cm (2½ ins) from beg, ending with a 2nd row and inc 15 sts evenly across last row. 60 (62, 64) sts.
Change to 4 mm (No. 8) needles. Cont in st st, inc 1 st at each end of 3rd row and foll 4th rows until there are 86 (94, 102) sts, then in foll 6th rows until there are 102 (106, 110) sts. Cont without shaping until

side edge measures 43 cm (17 ins) for **Women** or 48 cm (19 ins) for **Men**, ending with a purl row.

Shape top

Cast off 10 sts at beg of next 8 rows. Cast off rem sts.

Neckband

Using back-stitch, join shoulder seams. With right side facing, using set of 3.25 mm (No. 10) needles and MC, beg at left shoulder seam, knit up 96 (102, 108) sts evenly around neck edge, including sts from stitch holders.
1st Round: *K1, P1, rep from * to end.
Rep 1st round until neckband measures 5 cm (2 ins) from beg. Cast off **loosely** in rib.

To make up

Using back-stitch, sew in Sleeves placing centre top of Sleeve to shoulder seam. Join side and Sleeve seams. Fold Neckband in half onto wrong side and slip-stitch in position.

Djarram - Tree Bark Nets

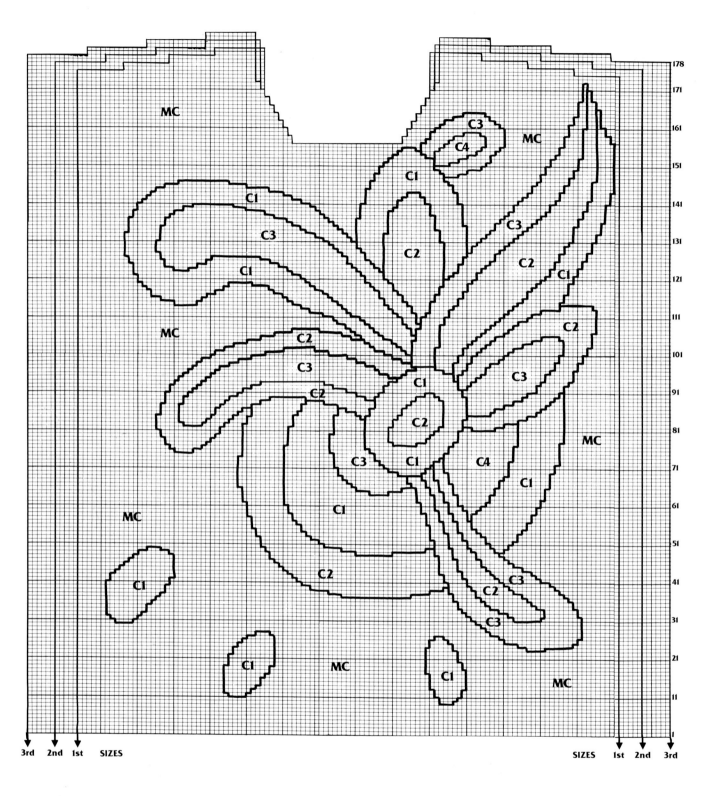

Rainstorm Magic

Rainstorm Magic

'These men are sitting down making rainstorm magic. They bring storm clouds and lightning over, bringing the rain.'

The rainy season in the north brings new growth, new foods and tells the people that it is time to move on in their seasonal nomadic migrations. Rainmaking is an important ritual in a dry country like Australia, and certain clever people, tribal 'doctors', have the ceremonial knowledge to bring rain, to summon the wrath of the Rainbow Serpent, an ancestral being who often dwells in waterholes and attracts the rainclouds.

Note: Before commencing the garment it is essential to check your tension (see below).

		S	M	L
To Fit	CM	76-81	86-91	97-102
Bust/Chest	INS	30-32	34-36	38-40
Actual	CM	106	116	127
Measurement	INS	42	46	50
Length to Back	CM	64	65	66
Neck (approx)	INS	25	25½	26

Note: This is a loose-fitting garment.

Materials

Cleckheaton Natural 8 Ply 50 g (2 oz) balls or equivalent yarn to give stated tension.

	S	M	L
MC (Rust)	8	9	10
C1 (Grey)	1	1	1
C2 (Sand)	1	1	1
C3 (Dark Brown)	1	1	1
C4 (Red)	1	1	1

1 pair each 4 mm (No. 8), 3.25 mm (No. 10) and 1 set of 3.25 mm (No. 10) knitting needles or, **the required size to give correct tension**; 1 stitch holder; bobbins.

Tension

This garment has been designed at a tension of 22 sts to 10 cm (4 ins) over st st, using 4 mm (No. 8) needles.

Back

Using 3.25 mm (No. 10) needles and MC, cast on 105 (115, 127) sts.
1st Row: K2, *P1, K1, rep from * to last st, K1.

2nd Row: K1, *P1, K1, rep from * to end.
Rep 1st and 2nd rows until band measures 6 cm (2½ ins) from beg, ending with a 2nd row and inc 13 sts evenly across last row. 118 (128, 140) sts.
Change to 4 mm (No. 8) needles. Cont in st st (1 row K, 1 row P) until work measures 18.5 cm (7½ ins) from beg, ending with a purl row.** Work 48 rows st st.

Shape armholes

Cast off 9 (10, 12) sts at beg of next 2 rows. Dec 1 st at each end of next and foll alt rows until 84 (88, 92) sts rem. Work 53 (51, 49) rows.

Shape shoulders

Cast off 8 (8, 9) sts at beg of next 4 rows, then 8 (9, 8) sts at beg of foll 2 rows. Leave rem 36 (38, 40) sts on a stitch holder.

Front

Work as for Back to **.
Next Row: K81 (86, 92) MC, work 1st row of Graph, K31 (36, 42) MC.
Next Row: P29 (34, 40) MC, work 2nd row of Graph, P79 (84, 90) MC.
Next Row: K78 (83, 89) MC, work 3rd row of Graph, K28 (33, 39) MC.
Next Row: P27 (32, 38) MC, work 4th row of Graph, P77 (82, 88) MC.
Work a further 40 rows from Graph as placed in last 4 rows.

Divide for 'V' neck

Left side of neck

Using MC,
Next Row: K59 (64, 70), **turn**. Dec 1 st at end (neck edge) in 2nd row. Work 1 row. 58 (63, 69) sts.

Shape armhole

Next Row: Cast off 9 (10, 12) sts, knit to last 0 (2, 2) sts, K0 (2, 2) tog. Dec 1 st at armhole edge in foll alt rows 8 (10, 12) times, **at same time** dec 1 st at neck edge in 2nd (4th, 2nd) row and foll 4th rows until 24 (25, 26) sts rem. Work 3 rows.

Shape shoulder

Cast off 8 (8, 9) sts at beg of next row and foll alt row. Work 1 row. Cast off.

Right side of neck

Join yarn to rem sts at right neck edge and keeping Graph correct work to end of row. Keeping Graph correct dec 1 st at beg (neck edge) of 2nd row, **2nd and 3rd Sizes Only** — and foll alt row. Work 2 (0, 0) rows from Graph.

Shape armhole

Cast off 9 (10, 12) sts at beg of next row. Keeping Graph correct, dec 1 st at armhole edge in next and foll alt rows 8 (10, 12) times in all, **at same time** dec 1 st at neck edge in next (3rd, next) row and foll 4th rows until 24 (25, 26) sts rem, noting that

when Graph has been completed to cont in MC and st st. Work 4 rows.

Shape shoulder

Complete to correspond with left shoulder.

Neckband

Using back-stitch, join shoulder seams. With right side facing, using set of 3.25 mm (No. 10) needles and MC, beg at left shoulder seam, knit up 75 (77, 79) sts evenly along left side of neck, pick up loop which lies before next st and mark with a coloured thread, (centre st), knit up 75 (77, 79) sts evenly along right side of neck, then knit across sts from back neck stitch holder, dec 1 st in centre. 186 (192, 198) sts.
1st Round: *P1, K1 rep from * to end.
2nd Round: Rib to within 2 sts of centre st, ybk, sl 1, K1, psso, K1, (centre st), K2tog, rib to end.
3rd Round: Rib to within 2 sts of centre st, P2togtbl, K1 (centre st), P2tog, rib to end.
Rep 2nd and 3rd rounds until neckband measures 2 cm (1 in) from beg. Cast off **loosely** in rib.

Armbands

With right side facing, using 3.25 mm (No. 10) needles and MC, knit up 111 (115, 121) sts evenly along armhole edge. Cont in rib as for lower band of Back, (beg with a 2nd row) until band measures 2 cm (1 in) from beg, ending with a 2nd row. Cast off **loosely** in rib.

To make up

Using back-stitch, join side and Armband seams.

Rainstorm Magic

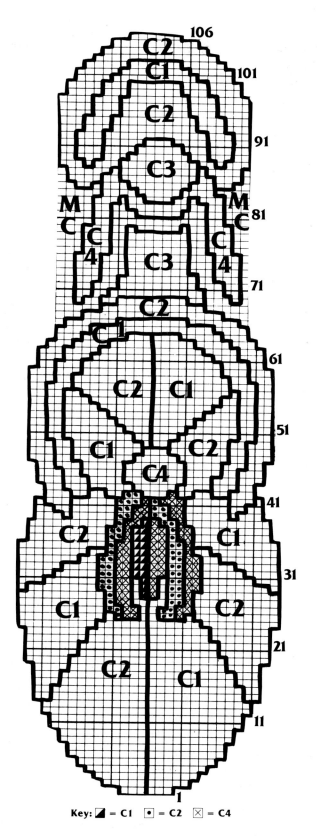

Key: ◤ = C1   ▫ = C2   ⊠ = C4

Kingirama - Grinding Stones

Kingirama - Grinding Stones

'Each family has its own grinding stones and only members of that family are allowed to use them. Different stones are used for grinding food, ochre, shaping spears and stone tools. The top grinding stone is called kingirama and men and women have their own bottom stone for their personal use. The man's stone is called angungorongoridja and the women's kungorongoridja.'

In this traditional design the stones are the round objects joined up by 'tracks'. Grinding stones are not carried around by the people, but left at the campsite for the following season when the family returns looking for food.

Note: Before commencing the garment it is essential to check your tension (see below).

To Fit		S	M	L
To Fit	CM	76-81	86-91	97-102
Bust/Chest	INS	30-32	34-36	38-40
Actual	CM	106	116	127
Measurement	INS	42	46	50
Length to Back	CM	64	65	66
Neck (approx)	INS	25	25½	26
Sleeve Seam				
Women (approx)	CM	43	43	43
	INS	17	17	17
Men (approx)	CM	48	48	48
	INS	19	19	19

Note: This is a loose-fitting garment.

Materials

Cleckheaton 8 Ply Machine Wash 50 g (2 oz) balls **or equivalent yarn to give stated tension.**

	S	M	L
MC (Black)	12	13	14
C1 (Blue)	1	1	1
C2 (Yellow)	1	1	1
C3 (Red)	1	1	1
C4 (Purple)	1	1	1
C5 (Pink)	1	1	1
C6 (Green)	1	1	1
C7 (White)	1	1	1

Note: You may require an extra ball of MC for men's sizes.
1 pair each 4 mm (No. 8) and 3.25 mm (No. 10), and 1 set of 3.25 mm (No. 10) knitting needles, or **the required size to give correct tension;** 2 stitch holders; bobbins.

Tension

This garment has been designed at a tension of 22 sts to 10 cm (4 ins) over st st, using 4 mm (No. 8) needles.

Front

Using 3.25 mm (No. 10) needles and MC, cast on 103 (113, 125) sts.
1st Row: K2, *P1, K1, rep from * to last st, K1.
2nd Row: K1, *P1, K1, rep from * to end.
Rep 1st and 2nd rows until band measures 8 cm (3 ins) from beg, ending with a 2nd row and inc 16 sts evenly across last row. 119 (129, 141) sts.
Change to 4 mm (No. 8) needles and beg patt.** Work 4 rows st st (1 row K, 1 row P). Work rows 1 to 132 inclusive from Graph, (C7 may be embroidered on afterwards using knitting stitch if desired). Using MC, work 6 (6, 8) rows st st.

Shape neck

Next Row: K48 (53, 58), turn. Dec 1 st at left neck edge in alt rows 6 (7, 7) times. 42 (46, 51) sts. Work 5 (5, 7) rows.

Shape shoulders

Cast off 11 (12, 13) sts at beg of next row and foll alt row, then 10 (11, 13) sts at beg of foll alt row. Work 1 row. Cast off. Slip next 23 (23, 25) sts onto a stitch holder and leave. Join yarn to rem sts and complete right hand side of neck to correspond with left side.

Back

Work as for Front to **. Cont in st st until Back measures same as Front to shoulder shaping, ending with a purl row.

Shape shoulders

Cast off 11 (12, 13) sts at beg of next 4 (4, 6) rows, then 10 (11, 12) sts at beg of foll 4 (4, 2) rows. Leave rem 35 (37, 39) sts on a stitch holder.

Sleeves

Using 3.25 mm (No. 10) needles and MC, cast on 43 (45, 47) sts. Work in rib as for lower band of Front until band measures 8 cm (3 ins) from beg, ending with a 2nd row and inc 14 sts evenly across last row. 57 (59, 61) sts.
Change to 4 mm (No. 8) needles. Cont in st st inc 1 st at each end of 5th and foll 4th rows until there are 95 (103, 111) sts,

1st and 2nd Sizes Only — cont inc foll 6th rows until there are 103 (107, 111) sts. Cont without shaping until side edge measures 43 cm (17 ins) for **Women** or 48 cm (19 ins) for **Men** from beg, ending with a purl row.

Shape top

Cast off 10 sts at beg of next 8 rows.
Cast off rem sts.

Neckband

Using back-stitch, join shoulder seams. With right side facing, using set of 3.25 mm (No. 10) needles and MC, knit up 92 (98, 106) sts evenly around neck edge, including sts from stitch holders.
1st Round: *K1, P1, rep from * to end.
Rep 1st round 9 times. Cast off **loosely** in rib.

To make up

Using back-stitch, sew in Sleeves placing centre top of Sleeve to shoulder seam. Join side and Sleeve seams. Using C7 and knitting stitch, embroider 'Desert Designs' on Front of Jumper if desired.

Kingirama - Grinding Stones

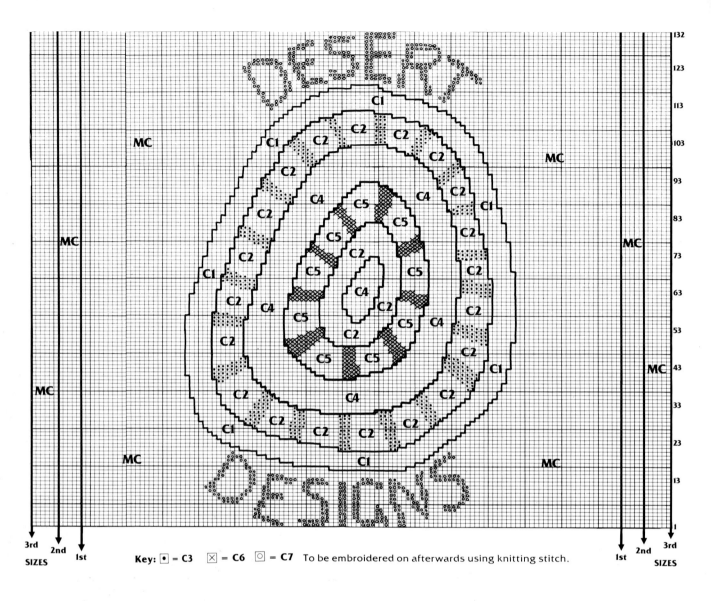

Key: ● = C3   ☒ = C6   ◎ = C7   To be embroidered on afterwards using knitting stitch.

Batjikala - The Totems

Batjikala - The Totems

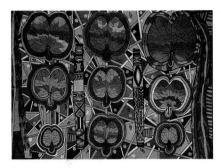

'When the pipe is made, it is then decorated with the family and clan designs, some of which can tell a small story.'

The pipe designs are the totems of different sections within the tribe. Totemic designs are meaningful in that they indicate the different duties and privileges of each group within the tribe.

Note: Before commencing the garment it is essential to check your tension (see below).

		S	M	L
To Fit	CM	76-81	86-91	97-102
Bust/Chest	INS	30-32	34-36	38-40
Actual	CM	106	116	127
Measurement	INS	42	46	50
Length to Back	CM	68	69	70
Neck (approx)	INS	27	27	27½
Sleeve Seam				
Women (approx)	CM	43	43	43
	INS	17	17	17
Men (approx)	CM	48	48	48
	INS	19	19	19

Note: This is a loose-fitting garment.

Materials

Cleckheaton Natural 8 Ply 50 g (2 oz) balls or equivalent yarn to give stated tension.

	S	M	L
MC (Rust)	10	11	12
C1 (Brown)	2	2	2
C2 (Grey)	1	1	1
C3 (Cream)	2	2	2
C4 (Black)	1	1	1
C5 (Sand)	1	1	1

Note: You may require an extra ball of MC for men's sizes.
1 pair each 4 mm (No. 8) and 3.25 mm (No. 10) knitting needles, or **the required size to give correct tension**; 1 stitch holder; bobbins; 8 buttons.

Tension

This garment has been designed at a tension of 22 sts to 10 cm (4 ins) over st st, using 4 mm (No. 8) needles.

Back

Using 3.25 mm (No. 10) needles and MC, cast on 105 (115, 127) sts.
1st Row: K2, *P1, K1, rep from * to last st, K1.

2nd Row: K1, *P1, K1, rep from * to end.
Rep 1st and 2nd rows until band measures 6 cm (2½ ins) from beg, ending with a 2nd row and inc 13 sts evenly across last row. 118 (128, 140) sts.
Change to 4 mm (No. 8) needles. Work 174 (176, 178) rows st st (1 row K, 1 row P).

Shape shoulders

Cast off 10 (11, 13) sts at beg of next 6 rows, then 11 (12, 11) sts at beg of foll 2 rows. Leave rem 36 (38, 40) sts on a stitch holder.

Left front

Using 3.25 mm (No. 10) needles and MC, cast on 53 (59, 65) sts.
Work in rib as for lower band of Back, until band measures 6 cm (2½ ins) from beg, ending with a 2nd row and inc 6 (5, 5) sts evenly across last row. 59 (64, 70) sts. Change to 4 mm (No. 8) needles. Work rows 1 to 157 inclusive from Graph A, for Left Front.

Shape neck

Keeping Graph correct, cast off 9 sts at beg of next row. Dec 1 st at neck edge in **every** row until 41 (45, 50) sts rem. Work 7 (8, 9) rows from Graph.

Shape shoulder

Cast off 10 (11, 13) sts at beg of next and foll alt rows 3 times in all. Work 1 row. Cast off.

Right front

Work to correspond with Left Front, following Graph A as indicated for Right Front.

Sleeves

Using 3.25 mm (No. 10) needles and MC, cast on 45 (47, 49) sts.
Work in rib as for lower band of Back until band measures 6 cm (2½ ins) from beg, ending with a 2nd row and inc 15 sts evenly across last row. 60 (62, 64) sts. Change to 4 mm (No. 8) needles. Cont in st st inc 1 st at each end of 3rd row and foll 4th rows until there are 86 (94, 102) sts, then in foll 6th rows until there are 102 (106, 110) sts. Cont without shaping until side edge measures 43 cm (17 ins) for **Women** or 48 cm (19 ins) for **Men**, from beg, ending with a purl row.

Shape top

Cast off 10 sts at beg of next 8 rows. Cast off rem sts.

Buttonhole bands

Right front band for women, left front band for men

Using 3.25 mm (No. 10) needles and MC, cast on 11 sts.
1st Row: K2, (P1, K1) 4 times, K1.
2nd Row: (K1, P1) 5 times, K1.
3rd Row: Rib 5, cast off 2 sts, rib 4.

4th Row: Rib 4, cast on 2 sts, rib 5.
Work 24 rows rib. Rep last 26 rows 5 times, then 3rd and 4th rows once. 7 buttonholes. Work 22 rows rib. ** Break off yarn, leave sts on a spare needle.

Left front band for women, right front band for men

Work as for other front band omitting buttonholes to **. Do not break off yarn. Leave sts on needle.

Neckband

Using back-stitch, join shoulder seams. With right side facing, using 3.25 mm (No. 10) needles and MC, rib across 11 sts on Right Front Band, knit up 93 (99, 105) sts evenly around neck edge, including sts from back neck stitch holder, then rib across Left Front Band sts. 115 (121, 127) sts. Work 9 rows rib as for lower band of Back, beg with a 2nd row of rib and working a buttonhole (as before) in 2nd and 3rd rows of Neckband. Cast off **loosely** in rib.

To make up

Using back-stitch, sew in Sleeves placing centre top of Sleeve to shoulder seam. Join side and Sleeve seams. Sew Front Bands in position stretching slightly to fit. Sew on buttons.

Batjikala - The Totems

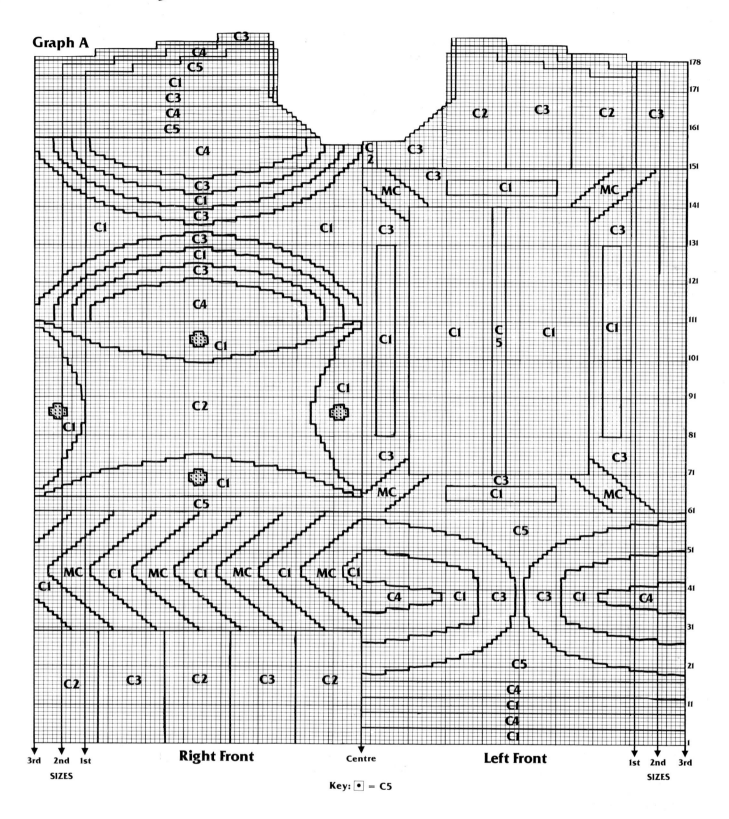